TWENTIETH CENTURY INTERPRETATIONS
OF

# KEATS'S ODES

*A Collection of Critical Essays*

Edited by
JACK STILLINGER

Prentice-Hall, Inc.　A SPECTRUM BOOK　*Englewood Cliffs, N. J.*

Current printing (last number):

10   9   8   7   6   5   4   3   2

PRENTICE-HALL INTERNATIONAL, INC. (*London*)

# Contents

# Introduction:
# Imagination and Reality in
# the Odes of Keats

## by Jack Stillinger

John Keats was twenty-three years old when, in the spring and autumn of 1819, he wrote the five odes that are the subjects of these critical essays. He had begun serious composition little more than three years earlier, had published a first volume, *Poems* (1817), and a long narrative poem, *Endymion* (1818), in the two years preceding, and would publish only one more volume, containing the odes and, as the title page has it, *Lamia, Isabella, The Eve of St. Agnes, and Other Poems* (1820), before his death in 1821 at the age of twenty-five. When it was all over, he had the shortest writing career—a span (not counting juvenile effusions) of four years, from the winter of 1815–16 to the end of 1819—of any of the major poets in English, and without question the rapidest development.

It is a nice job to explain that development. The documents concerning the facts of his early life—the upbringing around a London livery stable, enrollment at John Clarke's academy at Enfield, a few miles north of London, when he was seven, the death of his father and hasty remarriage of his mother when he was eight, the death of his mother when he was fourteen—contain no hint of the poet-to-be. His formal education, first at Clarke's school (1803–11), then as an apprentice to an apothecary-surgeon of Edmonton (1811–15), and finally as a medical student at Guy's Hospital, from which after a year's course he emerged in 1816 with a certificate to practice as an apothecary, was meager by the standards of the time for a man of letters. We know that he read widely, in the Latin and English poets, under Clarke's tutelage and on his own. It is not difficult, especially as we see it dramatized in the *Poems* of 1817, to understand his desire to be a poet. But it borders on the impossible, once Keats has embarked on his choice, to account fully for the incredibly fast ripening in his work from the earliest imitative efforts, embarrassing in their lushness and sentimentality, to the richest products of his maturity. One can observe, at any stage in their careers, how a Ben Jonson, a Tennyson, or even a Pope *crafted* his poems. With Keats, just as with Shakespeare, one wants, even while knowing better, to invoke the mystery and magic associated with "genius" to say what lay behind the fusion of serious theme with the perfectly controlled sounds and abundance of striking images that we see in his finest writing.

One can, however, describe what Keats's poems are about, and in the description at least partially account for his peculiar excellence. He wrote on most of the standard subjects: nature, poetry, art, love, fame, and death. But in the over-all view, his significant poems center on a single basic problem, the mutability inherent in nature and human life, and openly or in disguise they debate the pros and cons of a single hypothetical solution, transcendence of earthly limitations by means of the visionary imagination. If one were to summarize the career in a single sentence, it would be something like this: Keats came to learn that the kind of imagination he pursued was a false lure, inadequate to the needs of the problem, and in the end he traded the visionary for the naturalized imagination, embracing experience and process as his own and man's chief good. His honesty in treating the problem and his final opting for the natural world, where all the concrete images of poetry come from and where melodies impinge on "the sensual ear" or not at all, are what, more than anything else, guarantee his place "among the English Poets."

## *I. The Structure and Theme of the Odes*

What goes up must, in reality, come down. Stock notions of "romanticism" to the contrary, the typical lyric of the English Romantic period has the structure of a literal or metaphorical excursion that can best be represented, in blackboard fashion, by the following diagram:

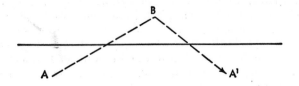

The horizontal line stands for a boundary separating the actual world (below) and the ideal (above). (The two realms have many common labels: earth and heaven, mortality and immortality, time and eternity, materiality and spirituality, the known and the unknown, the finite and the infinite, realism and romance, and so on. The ideal is represented above the line because it is, so to speak, a "higher" reality —what is intended by the difference between "natural" and "*super*-natural.") Characteristically, the speaker in a Romantic lyric begins in the real world (A), takes off in mental flight to visit the ideal (B), and then—for a variety of reasons, but most often because he finds something wanting in the imagined ideal or because, being a native of the real world, he discovers that he does not or cannot belong permanently in the ideal—returns home to the real (A$^1$). But he has not simply arrived back where he began (hence "A$^1$" rather than "A" at the descent), for he has acquired something—a better understanding of a situation, a change in attitude toward it—from the experience of the flight, and he is never again quite the same person who spoke at the beginning of the poem.

In various ways, hundreds of poems, and not all of them lyrics, may be seen to display this typical structure—to pick examples almost at random, Coleridge's *The Eolian Harp* (mental fantasies leading up to a "what if" speculation about the organic unity of "all of animated nature," followed by a descent to orthodoxy at the end), *The Rime of the Ancient Mariner* (a voyage out to the unknown and subsequent journey home to the real world and society), and poems by Wordsworth as diverse as *A Slumber Did My Spirit Seal* (slumber succeeded by awakening, a return of sorts), *Tintern Abbey* (the general progress is from memory to the awareness of "A presence . . . something far more deeply interfused," and then back to memory), *Ode: Intimations of Immortality* (an imaginative excursion to childhood's "visionary gleam" and what it intimates, followed by a return to the adult world of "the light of common day"), all those poems in which a fancied notion is put down by a closer look (e.g., *Resolution and Independence* and *A Narrow Girdle of Rough Stones*), and even the Prologue to *Peter Bell,* where a literal flight among the stars proves a terrifying experience for the poet. Many others could be cited, and the structure is of course common to other literatures and art besides that of the early nineteenth century. In *The Wizard of Oz,* Dorothy's "homeward fever" (to borrow a phrase from *Endymion*) is no different from that experienced by a number of cosmically displaced Romantic heroes, and the lesson she learns at the end, "There's no place like home," is a main point, though never in quite such plain language, of some notable poems of Keats's period.

It is not really necessary to place Keats historically—in any sense in which he is "romantic" we are still today in the same "romantic movement"—but it happens that the structure embraces two dominant tendencies in the literature of his time, the desire to transcend the world of flux and the desire to merge with that world, and it helps explain the way in which both of these contradictory tendencies may exist, as they so often do, in the same work. Take Keats's *Bright Star* sonnet as a simple case in point:[1]

> Bright star! would I were steadfast as thou art—
>     Not in lone splendour hung aloft the night
> And watching, with eternal lids apart,
>     Like nature's patient, sleepless Eremite,
> The moving waters at their priestlike task
>     Of pure ablution round earth's human shores,
> Or gazing on the new soft fallen mask
>     Of snow upon the mountains and the moors—
> No—yet still steadfast, still unchangeable,
>     Pillow'd upon my fair love's ripening breast,
> To feel for ever its soft fall and swell,
>     Awake for ever in a sweet unrest,
> Still, still to hear her tender-taken breath,
> And so live ever—or else swoon to death.

In terms of the blackboard diagram, the leap from A to B is made in the first line, as the speaker focuses his imagination on a star and its steadfastness. Lines 2–8 explore (and already with "Not" in l. 2 begin to reject) the unearthliness of the star's situation: it shines in "*lone* splendour," is aloof, never sleeps, is associated with a cold and inhuman religious asceticism, and is separated by a considerable distance from the beauties of nature. The sestet makes it clear that the speaker desires this steadfastness not "aloft" but on earth, in his own world of love and movement, "ripening" and "sweet unrest," and that this is the only kind of steadfastness he will settle for ("or else swoon to death"). Thus the speaker has chosen a symbol of unearthly permanence, has stripped away its unearthly qualities, and has concluded by bringing what he wants of the symbol—really the bare notion of steadfastness with which he started—home to the mortal world.

It is a short poem, and the lesson the speaker learns from his imaginative flight—perhaps that the steadfastness of a star is acceptable only with considerable qualification—does not greatly enlarge his understanding (his mind is made up from l. 2 on). But in its preoccupation with time and timelessness, both out of the world and in it, and in its movement of excursion and return, the sonnet epitomizes the principal theme and structure common to the odes. If we ignore

[1] Here, as in my discussion of the odes more generally, I am indebted especially to David Perkins, whose three chapters on Keats in *The Quest for Permanence* (Cambridge, Mass., 1959) still seem the best short account of the poet's principal concerns, attitudes, and methods.

(as, for the sake of brevity, I must ignore) most of the subtleties and complexities that make them the great poems that they are, the odes as a group may be read as an investigation of the imagination's ability to cope with time and change: the first three are mainly exploratory, and the final two are written, as it were, with the exploration over and an awareness of the results. And they are all in some degree relatable to the structure I have been discussing: *Nightingale* and *Grecian Urn* follow the pattern of flight and return all the way through, and the others may be thought of as partial exemplifications, centering on the excursion (*Psyche*) or the return (*Melancholy* and *Autumn*).

*Ode to Psyche,* apparently the earliest of the five odes to be written,[2] is the least clearly organized of the poems and the least easy to integrate with the others in any unified view. It is, more than anything else, a poem about mental life in the modern world, and as such it picks up the theme of Keats's dedicatory sonnet *To Leigh Hunt, Esq.* in the 1817 volume, which opens with the statement that "Glory and loveliness have passed away" and goes on to establish the idea— which could serve as one capsule summary of the Romantic movement—that it is up to the poet himself to compensate for the cruel banishment of fairies, gods, myth, and religion by Lockian and Newtonian "cold philosophy." In the ode, the speaker describes Psyche's (and his own) time as an age

> too late for antique vows,
> Too, too late for the fond believing lyre,
> When holy were the haunted forest boughs,
> Holy the air, the water, and the fire                    (36–39)

—an age "so far retir'd / From happy pieties" (40–41). In the face of such impoverishment, declaring that he himself will be Psyche's priest, the speaker takes an excursive leap to "some untrodden region of my mind," where he will "build a fane" to worship her (50–51). The poem is the most ambiguous of the odes, and the concluding specula-

---

[2] Four of the five odes can be dated with a fair degree of certainty. *Psyche* was completed by April 30, 1819 (*The Letters of John Keats,* ed. Hyder E. Rollins [Cambridge, Mass., 1958], II, 106–8); *Nightingale* and *Grecian Urn* are both dated May in the transcripts; *To Autumn* was written on September 19 (*Letters,* II, 167). Although *Melancholy* is generally assigned to May, there is actually no evidence for dating it except for its thematic and stylistic similarity to other work of the spring, summer, and autumn of 1819. I should explain that I have omitted *Ode on Indolence,* sometimes classed with the others as the sixth "great ode," on the grounds of its obvious inferiority as a poem. It lacks the dramatic tension that characterizes the first four of the odes (all but *To Autumn*), and the sharpness of imagery of all five. The omission of the poem from the *Lamia* volume of 1820 suggests that Keats himself recognized its inferiority. Several other "odes" among Keats's poems are also excluded from consideration here.

tions about the higher reality that the speaker looks forward to can
be read in two different ways—either as an affirmation of the successful working of the imagination to recreate lost glory and loveliness
(in such a view the imagination would be more akin to Wordsworthian creative sensibility than to the visionary faculty of Keats's
other poems), or as a retreat in which the powers of the mind provide
only a partial solution. As David Perkins has pointed out,[3] there are
various hints of insubstantiality—the "stars without a name" (61), the
idea of *feigning* (62), and the questionable delight of "shadowy
thought" (65), contrasting strikingly with the luxurious physicality
of Cupid's and Psyche's lovemaking in the opening stanza of the poem
—that suggest something less than a triumphant solving of the problem at the end. It may be that the hypothetical excursion to "some
untrodden region of my mind" leaves the poet stranded, and at too
great a distance from the forest and bedded grass where he last saw
the lovers; whatever the nature of the perception in the opening
stanza—waking dream or "thoughtless" vision (see l. 7)—the "working
brain" and "shadowy thought" of the final lines do not seem an entirely satisfactory compensation.

*Ode to a Nightingale* is the first of the odes to bring the speaker
back to reality. In the opening three stanzas, he yearns after an invisible bird and the condition it symbolizes, an ideal state trancend-
ing the mortal world of weariness, fever, and fret, "Where youth
grows pale, and spectre-thin, and dies . . . Where Beauty cannot
keep her lustrous eyes," and so on (23–30). By the middle of the
fourth stanza, he succeeds in joining the bird by means of imagination, "the viewless wings of Poesy" (33). Almost immediately, however
—just as when the "exil'd mortal" Endymion first discovers himself
cut off from familiar surroundings (*End.*, II, 285–332)—there follows
the speaker's vivid realization of what he has lost by crossing the
boundary into an imagined ideal: "But here [i.e., in the forest] there
is no light . . . . I cannot see what flowers are at my feet," nor any
of a series of lovingly detailed images drawn from memory of the
transient natural world that he has left behind and now longs for
(38–50). The rest of the poem represents an ever-widening separation
between speaker and bird. In the sixth stanza, the idea of the richness
of death is nullified by the speaker's abrupt awareness that he would
become a lifeless sod. The seventh stanza, spoken with full knowledge
of the difference between mortal speaker and "immortal Bird," puts
the nightingale further and further out of the realm of ordinary life,
associating it with medieval times ("emperor and clown"), Biblical
history ("the sad heart of Ruth," in "alien" surroundings), and finally

---

[3] See the paragraph by Perkins included below in "View Points."

"faery lands forlorn," where there is no human life at all. In the final stanza, the speaker returns to himself and the real world. The nightingale is suddenly divested of its symbolism as it flies off and the speaker locates it, not in another ideal forest, but in the familiar landscape of "the near meadows . . . the still stream . . . the hill-side . . . the next valley-glades" (76–78). Where before the bird had been "immortal" and the speaker "in embalmed darkness" had longed for death, now the voice of the bird is "buried deep" (77) and the speaker is very much alive. At the end of the poem he is back in the same world from which he took off, but he has learned some significant things in the interim about his own world, his condition in it, and his relationship to the hypothetical ideal symbolized by the bird. The nightingale has proved to be a "deceiving elf," the "fancy" (= imagination) "cheat[s]" (73–74), and he does not seem sorry to return from the final emptiness that he has discovered to be "forlorn."

In *Ode on a Grecian Urn*, whose movement parallels that of the preceding poem, the hypothetical ideal is the realm of art. The poem offers a beautifully clear example of the way in which meaning results from the structuring of attitudes, for, once the speaker is caught up in the life pictured on the urn (by the end of the first stanza), a seesaw opposition of earthly versus urnly values ensues (11–30) in which, up to a point, the decision could go either way. On the one hand, "Heard melodies are sweet," the piper cannot cease his piping (and may therefore get tired), the trees are confined to a single season, and the lover can never catch or kiss the maiden he is pursuing; on the other hand, "unheard" melodies "Are sweeter," the piper is "unwearied," the boughs are "happy" in their situation, and the lover and the maiden will love and be young and fair forever. The outcome of such an opposition depends of course on the order in which the pros and cons are presented: if B has X quality (good) and Y quality (bad), we can express either an essentially negative attitude ("although B is X, we mustn't overlook Y") or a positive one ("in spite of Y, B is very X") according to our arrangement of the facts. The view of life on the urn is favorable at the end of both the second stanza ("For ever wilt thou love, and she be fair!") and the third (the lovers on the urn are far above "All breathing human passion . . . That leaves . . . A burning forehead, and a parching tongue"). In the fourth stanza, however, the speaker takes a fresh look at the urn, and his attitude changes by implication to a final decision in favor of earthly life. The procession of priest, heifer, and townspeople is stopped forever midway between an attractive destination (a "green altar") and an attractive source (the "little town by river or sea shore, / Or mountain-built with peaceful citadel"), and the permanent emptiness of the unseen town strikes the speaker as unbearably sad:

> And, little town, thy streets for evermore
> Will silent be; and not a soul to tell
> Why thou art desolate, can e'er return.          (38–40)

The perpetual midwayness of the procession (similar to a state described as "Purgatory blind" in the verse epistle *To J. H. Reynolds, Esq.*, l. 80) reflects back on the situation of the piper, the lovers, and the trees, where process is frozen to a standstill and there is no fulfillment. "Desolate" in line 40 is the counterpart of "forlorn" in *Ode to a Nightingale*. It brings the speaker back to his sole self, and at the beginning of the final stanza he addresses the urn not as living entity but as artifact: it is now an "Attic shape," an "attitude," "overwrought" with "brede" of "marble" figures and trees, a "silent form," a "Cold Pastoral." Like the nightingale, it has offered a tentative ideal—momentarily "teas[ing]" the speaker "out of thought"—but has also led the speaker to understand the shortcomings of the ideal. The final lines present a special problem in interpretation (see the Appendix), but it is clear that, while the urn is not entirely rejected at the end, its value lies in its character as a work of art, not in its being a possible substitute for life in the actual world. However punctuated, the urn's "message" amounts to what the speaker has come to realize in his speculations—that the only beauty accessible to mortal man exists "on earth." The urn is "a friend to man" for helping him to arrive at this conclusion through just such ponderings as we have witnessed in the course of the poem.

*Ode on Melancholy*, the most logically constructed of the odes, instead of following the flight-and-return pattern of the two preceding poems, enjoins against making the trip. "Go *not* to Lethe": the first stanza tells what not to do "when the melancholy fit shall fall," and beginning with forgetfulness and progressing through narcotics to poisons and death the images represent various anodynes to escape the unhappiness of the mortal condition. (Flying off to join the nightingale in the forest and entering into the life on the urn are the counterparts in the poems just discussed.) The anodynes are rejected because they shut out pleasure as well as pain: "For shade to shade will come too drowsily, / And drown the wakeful anguish of the soul." The second stanza advises what to do instead:

> Then glut thy sorrow on a morning rose,
> Or on the rainbow of the salt sand-wave,
> Or on the wealth of globed peonies;
> Or if thy mistress some rich anger shows,
> Emprison her soft hand, and let her rave,
> And feed deep, deep upon her peerless eyes

—that is, seize and experience the beauty of the transient natural and human world as fully as one can. The third stanza gives the rationale for these prescriptions (and, for that matter, a "doctrinal" basis for the other odes and poems of 1819 more generally). The pleasures and pains of life are inextricably bound up together: beauty and the melancholy awareness that beauty must die, joy and the simultaneous fading of joy, "aching Pleasure" and its instant turning to poison— all are inseparable, and one either accepts the pleasure-pain complexity or renounces life altogether. Of the alternatives given—the insensibility of narcosis and death in the first stanza and the bursting of "Joy's grape against his palate fine" toward the end of the third— the latter is obviously to be preferred.

The last of the odes, and the least argumentative, though nonetheless deeply philosophical, *To Autumn* may be thought of as written out of the experience of the earlier poems. From beginning to end it celebrates the world of process—of "maturing," "ripeness," "budding" —not with innocent delight in the beauties of nature, but rather with a mature understanding that (to quote Wordsworth) this is "the very world, which is the world / Of all of us,—the place where, in the end, / We find our happiness, or not at all!" (*The Prelude*, XI, 142–44). A momentary yearning for the otherworlds of the nightingale and the urn is expressed at the beginning of the third stanza: "Where are the songs of Spring? Ay, where are they?" But it is immediately put down by the next line, "Think not of them, thou hast thy music too," and the remainder of the poem, even while hinting of death among the sounds of life, is unambiguously affirmative. The imagination is now devoted not to visionary flights but to a detailed examining of every natural sight and sound at hand, and the focus and attitude show the speaker reconciled to the real world he lives in.

## II. Keats's Development and the Context of the Odes

In explaining how Keats, at the age of twenty-three, arrived at the maturity he shows in the poems just discussed, it is not entirely fanciful to view his over-all development in terms of just such a structure as we have seen in the best of the odes—a beginning flight from the real toward the ideal, a thoroughgoing imaginative assessment of the ideal, and a final return to the real. The *Poems* of 1817—which are mainly about the question of whether Keats can and should be a poet, and which proceed from hesitancy to affirmation and the dedication to a ten-year program of development that, as it turns out, he had to condense into less than half that time—show many of the same thematic concerns that dominate the mature poems. There are above all the interest in perception and vision, the many contrasts of earthly and heavenly states, and the reiterated idea that imagination can serve as a bridge from one to the other. Keats first launches into vision in the twenty-ninth line of the opening poem (*I Stood Tip-toe*), and there are more ambitious excursions in the middle poem (the epistle *To My Brother George*) and the concluding piece (*Sleep and Poetry*). The attempts are sometimes tentative and awkward, but there is no doubt that in writing the poems Keats was (for poetic purposes at least) affirming literal belief in a commonplace of the day, the stock metaphor of visionary flight. (Compare, for an illuminating example, Leigh Hunt's *Politics and Poetics*, ll. 59–100, to see as cliché the kind of thing Keats was taking seriously.) Most of these poems were written in 1816, and in the pattern of Keats's career they may be taken collectively as fledgling ascent.

*Endymion,* which Keats began in April, 1817, a month after his first volume was published, and completed in first draft at the end of November of the same year, represents his longest excursion in the realm of the ideal. It is the poem he had to write in order to begin freeing himself of the stock belief that informs the early poems. The allegorical narrative, which up to a point follows the classical myth of Endymion and the moon-goddess Cynthia, and may be read in part as a reply to Shelley's *Alastor,* which was published in the year before, is basically a simple one: a shepherd prince becomes enamored of an unknown goddess who visits him in a dream; turning his back on the world, he sets forth in quest of a reunion with her, and wanders through caverns, under the ocean, and through the air; after several adventures, he meets and falls in love with an Indian maiden, and vows to give up his pursuit of the goddess—whereupon the maiden reveals that she is Cynthia in disguise, and the two are blissfully reunited. Into this story Keats weaves a complexity of themes: the idea of "fellowship with essence" (a kind of imaginative identification with things outside oneself that leads, at its highest reach, to union with the ideal); the conflict of solitude and self-love with humanitarian concerns; the opposing claims of human and immortal existence; and several others. In the first and fourth books, however, the overriding preoccupation is the question of the authenticity of dreams, which here as in most of Keats's subsequent poems are meant to symbolize the visionary imagination.

Toward the end of Book I, in an especially significant exchange with his worldly-minded sister, Peona, who wants him to give up his quest ("how light / Must dreams themselves be . . . . Why pierce high-fronted honour to the quick / For nothing but a dream?"—ll. 754–60), Endymion goes to great lengths to justify the reality of the dream he is bent on pursuing (ll. 769 ff.). Keats refers to this argument in a well-known letter to Benjamin Bailey (November 22, 1817) when he affirms his belief in "the authenticity of the Imagination"—"What the imagination seizes as Beauty must be truth . . . . The Imagination may be compared to Adam's dream [in *Paradise Lost*, VIII, 452–90] —he awoke and found it truth" (*Letters*, I, 184–85). Toward the end of his wanderings, however, Endymion has grave doubts:

> I have clung
> To nothing, lov'd a nothing, nothing seen
> Or felt but a great dream! . . .
> . . . gone and past
> Are cloudy phantasms. Caverns lone, farewell!
> And air of visions, and the monstrous swell
> Of visionary seas! No, never more
> Shall airy voices cheat me . . . .                    (IV, 636–54)

As a matter of biographical fact, Keats wrote these lines very shortly after sending the letter to Bailey. It is of course Endymion who is speaking, at the height of his perplexity in finding himself in love with both a visionary goddess and one who he thinks is a mortal maiden, but the genuine fervency of the denial contrasts sharply with the affirmation of certainty in the letter. Forced to choose between the earthly and the ideal, Endymion renounces the ideal, and is saved only when the two turn out to be the same. It seems clear that he had to come to terms with human existence before he could be "Ensky'd" at the end; on the evidence of the poem, the way to heaven lies in earthly, not visionary, experiences.

The year 1818 marks an important turning point in Keats's mental life. Though hints, and occasionally more than hints, of skepticism were written into the first draft of *Endymion*, it was in the winter of 1817–18 that Keats himself noticed what he described as "a little change . . . in my intellect lately" (*Letters*, I, 214). Already tired of the poem before he finished it, he grew increasingly discontented as he revised it and copied it out for the printer (between January and the middle of March, 1818),[4] and several influences combined to turn him further against the kind of romance it represented: conversation and correspondence with the serious-minded Bailey; careful reading of Wordsworth, whom he met in December, 1817; the attractiveness of the comic sense of Fielding and Smollett, and a new appreciation of the tragic sense of Shakespeare. The change shows itself in a number of short poems written during the winter, perhaps most

[4] See Glen O. Allen, "The Fall of Endymion: A Study in Keats's Intellectual Growth," *Keats-Shelley Journal*, VI (1957), 37–57.

notably in the sonnet *On Sitting Down to Read King Lear Once Again* (January), in which he dismisses "Romance" as a "barren dream." Toward the end of March, in the epistle *To J. H. Reynolds, Esq.*, he struggles with the relationship of imagination to "the lore of good and ill" and describes a terrifying vision he has had of nature's cruelty, "an eternal fierce destruction"; the middle section speaks of the inadequacy of dreaming, the failure of the visionary imagination, and Keats's inability to find a healthy alternative. Between February and April he wrote *Isabella,* in which courtly-love romance and the "simple plaining of a minstrel's song" give over to what Keats considered a tough-minded modern account of the "wormy circumstance" of Lorenzo's death and Isabella's derangement.[5] In the summer of this year his brother George emigrated to America, and Keats set out on a walking tour of the English Lakes and Scotland that exposed him not only to the glories of nature but to the realities of rural poverty. The serious poems written during this tour continue to worry about the imagination (in the sonnet *On Visiting the Tomb of Burns,* "Fickly imagination & sick pride" cast a "dead hue" upon "The real of Beauty" [6]) and to assert the impossibility of any permanent escape from the world—

> Scanty the hour and few the steps beyond the bourn of care,
> Beyond the sweet and bitter world,—beyond it unaware!
> Scanty the hour and few the steps, because a longer stay
> Would bar return, and make a man forget his mortal way:
> O horrible! . . .
> No, no, that horror cannot be, for at the cable's length
> Man feels the gentle anchor pull and gladdens in its strength.
>
> (*Lines Written in the Highlands,* ll. 29–40)

In the autumn Keats began work on the fragmentary epic *Hyperion,* which breaks off with the deification of Apollo—symbol of the humanitarian poet—through recognition and sympathetic understanding of the pain and misery of mortal life. At the beginning of December his brother Tom died.

The rapid growing-up that attended the intellectual and emotional experiences of 1818 goes far to account for what would otherwise be a paradox—that the more Keats saw of the sobering realities, the more favorable his attitude toward life in the world became as it is struc-

[5] See the present writer's "Keats and Romance," *Studies in English Literature,* VIII (1968), 593–605.

[6] I am quoting from the text established by J. C. Maxwell, "Keats's Sonnet on the Tomb of Burns," *Keats-Shelley Journal,* IV (1955), 77–80.

tured in his poems. The early work of 1816–17 (*Poems* and *Endymion*) proposed a visionary seeking after higher truth that we now view as romantic escapism. But as Keats confronted existence more openly, the simple escapism came to be rejected, and the poems of his maturity—by which one means those brilliant products, one after another, of a single year, 1819—pose serious conflicts that are resolved, when they are resolved at all, by acceptance of the pleasure-pain complexity of mortal life. Beginning in January, with *The Eve of St. Agnes*, which depicts the plight of a hoodwinked maiden who mistakenly thinks she can separate the pleasures from the pain of life by following a superstitious ritual and dreaming about them, Keats hit his stride. *The Eve of St. Agnes* was followed by *The Eve of Saint Mark* (February), in which another hoodwinked maiden similarly cuts herself off from the realities of life by investing all her interests and emotions in the legend of a long-dead martyr.[7] *La Belle Dame sans Merci* (April) shows a wretched knight-at-arms unable to recover from a ghastly visionary experience. Then in April and May come the odes—*Psyche, Nightingale, Grecian Urn,* and *Melancholy*. In the summer Keats wrote *Lamia,* in which still another hoodwinked dreamer, like all the others unable to shed his human nature, suffers frustration and death through his engrossment in a visionary ideal, as represented by his love affair with the snake-woman Lamia. *The Fall of Hyperion,* which Keats began in the summer and gave up late in September, two days after writing *To Autumn,* ends the year on the same note as it began, the dangers of dreaming: "The poet and the dreamer are distinct," Moneta tells the poet, in a passage that may serve as an epitome of the position Keats had arrived at— "Diverse, sheer opposite, antipodes. / The one pours out a balm upon the world, / The other vexes it" (I, 199–202). To carry out the analogy between the over-all career and the structure of his odes, Keats began his descent from the ideal in the winter of 1817–18, and by 1819 he was firmly grounded in the realities of the actual world. The central point of the poems of 1819, from *The Eve of St. Agnes* through *The Fall of Hyperion,* is that mortal man cannot escape his mortality, and that dreaming and the mental process it stands for, a too exclusive commitment to the visionary imagination, produce only unhappiness. Keats's dreamers of this year either come to grief through their delusions or they learn their lesson and wake up. In the best of the odes the dreamers wake up.

---

[7] I have discussed these poems in "The Hoodwinking of Madeline: Scepticism in 'The Eve of St. Agnes,'" *Studies in Philology,* LVIII (1961), 533–55, and "The Meaning of 'poor cheated soul' in Keats's 'The Eve of Saint Mark,'" *English Language Notes,* V (1968), 193–96.

A brief glance at the order of poems in Keats's final volume, published in July, 1820, may serve as a basis for summary. The contents are as follows:

| | |
|---|---|
| *Lamia* | *Ode* ["Bards of Passion and of |
| *Isabella* | Mirth"] |
| *The Eve of St. Agnes* | *Lines on the Mermaid Tavern* |
| *Ode to a Nightingale* | *Robin Hood* |
| *Ode on a Grecian Urn* | *To Autumn* |
| *Ode to Psyche* | *Ode on Melancholy* |
| *Fancy* | *Hyperion, a Fragment* |

Arranged as they are, the poems show a progressive abandonment of the ideal and acceptance of the natural world, and a gradual movement from irresolution to resolution. *Lamia* sets forth the concern of nearly the entire volume—a clear (and in this poem unreconcilable) opposition between the ideal and the real, with dreaming as a metaphor for the mortal Lycius' involvement in an illusory ideal. *Isabella* and *The Eve of St. Agnes* anticipate the attitude of poems to follow by bringing a realistic view of things to bear on "old Romance." *Ode to a Nightingale* pictures an imaginative and unsuccessful attempt to merge with the supernatural (the "immortal" nightingale is no natural bird until the very end, and as such it has the same status as the fairy-creatures and goddesses that bewitch other Keatsian dreamers from Endymion through the knight of *La Belle Dame* and Lycius—even Porphyro in *The Eve of St. Agnes* is associated with fairies and magic). *Ode on a Grecian Urn* shows the same attempt to escape into the realm of art, and *Ode to Psyche* (with its perhaps countering companion *Fancy*) projects an excursion into "some untrodden region" of the mind. The next three poems journey into the past as still another realm of escape, but the tone is light, and there is an awareness throughout that "those days are gone away" (*Robin Hood*). Then come the two final odes, *To Autumn* and *Melancholy,* with their focus on the natural world and unequivocal acceptance of it. Having rejected or found wanting the supernatural, art, the mind, and the past, the poet has only nature left; but the tone of these last poems makes clear that nature suffices. At the conclusion, as if to show what this maturing might have led to, *Hyperion* depicts the "dying into life" of the Apollo-poet through "Knowledge enormous" of the human condition. Apollo's reign, like Keats's career, is terminated just as it gets under way, and since Keats knew he was mortally ill when he assembled and arranged the poems for publication, it seems likely that he himself saw the parallel. The poem breaks off in mid-sentence, and we are left with a row and a half of asterisks, and then the two words, "The End."

## III. Keats's Reputation

Keats was not widely read in his own day. Chopped up by the *Blackwood's* and *Quarterly* reviewers (mainly because of his association with the political radical Leigh Hunt), he aimed for posterity and a circle of friends who, after his death, worked heroically to make his poetry better known. The publication of Richard Monckton Milnes's *Life, Letters, and Literary Remains, of John Keats* (1848), based on unpublished poems, letters, and reminiscences supplied by those friends, finally brought Keats a measure of the fame he deserved, and as his life and poems were read and reread in the latter half of the century he came to be nearly idolized by the Victorians. Generally he was admired for the wrong reasons, as a poet of art for art's sake, the sensualist poet, the painter of rich pictures and the burster of Joy's grape, sometimes even with cayenne pepper on his tongue. It is a view that one sees in serious criticism as late as a generation ago—for example, in H. W. Garrod's statement that "I think him the great poet he is only when the senses capture him, when he finds truth in beauty, that is to say, when he does not trouble to find truth at all"[8] —and in popular journalism even today. The Humanist critics of the 1920's included him in their attack on Romantic escapism, reading *Ode to a Nightingale* as if it ended in the middle of the fourth stanza and *Ode on a Grecian Urn* as if it ended with the third stanza. Then around 1925, when Amy Lowell's massive biography was published, to be followed in the next year by Clarence D. Thorpe's *The Mind of John Keats*, critics began giving serious attention to Keats the thinker: the letters on Imagination (November 22, 1817), Negative Capability (December 21, 27[?], 1817, October 27, 1818), life as a "Mansion of Many Apartments" (May 3, 1818), and the world as a "vale of Soul-making" (April 21, 1819) suddenly became important. Close reading by the New Critics in the 1930's and '40's further enhanced his stature, and fresh interpretations of the odes and other poems poured forth to lift him almost to metaphysical heights.

Keats's reputation, which continues to grow, has never been better. With the help of Douglas Bush, W. J. Bate, and others, we have learned to take a middle view between the sensualist and the idealist, seeing Keats primarily as humanist—the honest confronter of difficult human problems, and the one of all the Romantics who least took refuge in some outdated system in order to solve them. Keats read human nature accurately, and his best poems picture the truth of the mind's impassioned questing. "Some desire is necessary to keep

---

[8] *Keats*, 2nd edn. (Oxford, 1939), p. 61.

life in motion," pronounces Imlac, in one of those eternal verities of Johnson's *Rasselas* (ch. VIII). The nine words may be taken to explain why the situation on the Grecian urn is rejected, once the impossibility of fulfillment has been grasped. Wordsworth says the same thing in his apostrophe to Imagination in Book VI of *The Prelude*:

> With hope it is, hope that can never die,
> Effort, and expectation, and desire,
> And something evermore about to be.          (606–8)

Endymion's speech about the warrior who, as soon as he captures one "fancied city of delight," must immediately set about taking another, and then another, again makes the point:

> But this is human life: the war, the deeds,
> The disappointment, the anxiety,
> Imagination's struggles, far and nigh,
> All human; bearing in themselves this good,
> That they are still the air, the subtle food,
> To make us feel existence, and to show
> How quiet death is.                    (*End.*, II, 153–59)

And as Keats put it in prose, in a letter to Bailey of March 13, 1818, just as he was finishing the revision of *Endymion* and was well launched on that year of accelerated growing-up, "every mental pursuit takes its reality and worth from the ardour of the pursuer—being in itself a nothing" (*Letters*, I, 242). It is above all this ardent "mental pursuit" that we see in Keats's poems, and his steady understanding where the reality lies that we especially admire. In the end, the "sudden rightnesses" of the odes put the mind just where it should be, in that delicate balance (as Wallace Stevens describes it) "below which it cannot descend, / Beyond which it has no will to rise."

# PART ONE

*Interpretations*

# The *Ode to Psyche*

## *by Kenneth Allott*

*To Psyche* is the Cinderella of Keats's great odes, but it is hard to see why it should be so neglected, and at least two poets imply that the conventional treatment of the poem is shabby and undeserved. In his introduction to Keats (1895) Robert Bridges wrote of the "extreme beauty" of the ode's last stanza and ranked the whole poem above *On a Grecian Urn* (though not above *On Melancholy*),[1] and Mr. T. S. Eliot in an unregarded parenthesis in *The Use of Poetry and the Use of Criticism* (1933) has commented more boldly, "The Odes—especially perhaps the *Ode to Psyche*—are enough for his [Keats's] reputation." I sympathize with these views. *To Psyche* is neither unflawed nor the best of odes, but to me it illustrates better than any other Keats's possession of poetic power in conjunction with what was for him an unusual artistic detachment—besides being a remarkable poem in its own right. This may be another way of saying that it is the most architectural of the odes, as it is certainly the one that culminates most dramatically. Some of Keat's remarks about it are relevant here.

> The following Poem—the last I have written is the first and the only one with which I have taken even moderate pains. I have for the most part dash'd of[f] my lines in a hurry. This I have done leisurely—I think it reads the more richly for it and will I hope encourage me to write other thing[s] in even a more peac[e]able and healthy spirit.[2]

Keats almost certainly wrote this before he wrote *To a Nightingale*, *On a Grecian Urn* and *On Melancholy*, and it is possible that he felt

---

"*The* Ode to Psyche" *by Kenneth Allott. From* John Keats: A Reassessment, *edited by Kenneth Muir (Liverpool University Press, 1958), pp. 74–94. Reprinted (with the omission of a brief section indicated by asterisks) by permission of the author and the Liverpool University Press.*

[1] *Collected Essays and Papers*, I.

[2] *Letters*, ed. M. B. Forman (1935), pp. 339-40—Letter 123, to George and Georgiana Keats, April 30, 1819.

later that these remaining Spring odes were written in a peaceable and healthy spirit. On balance this seems unlikely: *To Autumn* is the only other ode one would expect him to characterize in these terms. The "peaceable and healthy spirit" of *To Psyche* can be explained by saying that Keats is more engaged as an artist and less directly engaged as a man in this poem (in spite of its superficial blemishes) than in *To a Nightingale*, and the unexpected degree of aesthetic distance is probably connected with his "pains." Those which can be subsumed under "metrical preoccupation" have been fully discussed by Dr. Garrod and later by Mr. M. R. Ridley, but I suspect that Keats found a main difficulty in keeping his opulence from appearing obtrusive in what was for him a strain of unusually premeditated art. Apart from one or two lapses (mostly in the first stanza) I think he was successful—judged, that is to say, by the standards of success appropriate to the odes, which involve a somewhat different kind of expectation, as Matthew Arnold knew, from that with which one would read *King Lear* or the *Agamemnon*.[3] What I feel very strongly is that *To a Nightingale* should not be quoted to exemplify Keats's control of his poetic gift unless we are ready to disregard the difference between swimming powerfully but hypnotically with the tide of feeling and being able when necessary to make use of its force to come ashore roughly where one has planned. To change the metaphor, *To a Nightingale* and *On a Grecian Urn* have in common a pattern suggesting mounting sexual excitement and its relief—the point being that at an early stage in these poems the poet ceases to choose where he is going. This is not true of *To Psyche*, for which, as I have already said, an architectural metaphor seems best.

> Yes, I will be thy priest, and build a fane
>   In some untrodden region of my mind . . . .

The poem itself is a Corinthian detail in the "fane" promised to the goddess. Possibly such considerations were in Mr. Eliot's mind when he spoke of the ode: he may have felt, as I do, that Keats's artistry was more in evidence away from the empathic somnambulisms of the Urn and the Nightingale. Responsible critics of Keats such as Mr. Middleton Murry and Sir Herbert Read might well dissent from this position and find the "true voice of feeling" more distinctly in *To a Nightingale* than in *To Psyche*. Yet both these critics would probably agree that there is more detachment in the less-familiar ode, and it gives the poem a peculiar interest. Of course why *To*

---

[3] See the conclusion to Arnold's essay on Keats in *Essays in Criticism,* 2nd Series (1888).

*Psyche* should "hit so hard" [4] is left unexplained by these remarks, and to understand how our feelings have been engaged we need to go much further into it. I say "our feelings" because many readers seem to rise from the poem in the perplexed frame of mind honestly expressed by Mr. Graham Hough in some sentences from his recent handbook, *The Romantic Poets* (1953).

> The *Ode to Psyche* seems . . . the most purely fanciful [of the odes]. It would be easy to take it as a piece of lovely decorative mythology: but it is probably something more.[5]

Other readers must also have pondered the adequacy of Wordsworth's phrase for the invocation of Pan in *Endymion* ("A pretty piece of paganism") as a description of *To Psyche*, and felt with Mr. Hough that it would not quite do. When Mr. Hough tries to tell us what this "something more" may be, he is less happy.

> . . . the last stanza . . . is not merely a piece of fanciful devotion to an obsolete myth; but a recognition by Keats that his own exploration is to be of the interior landscape, that his ultimate devotion is to be neither to the objective world, nor to any power outside himself.

I find the last stanza less confusing than this explanation of it, and I do not think its meaning can be stated so compendiously.

Before turning to my own analysis of *To Psyche* I need to support the charge that the poem has suffered from being discussed in the course of scrutiny of the odes as a group of poems whose interest is assumed to lie in one or other of two directions—either in the individual quality of the poems commonly regarded as the most important, or in the unique nature of some group-character which the critic is bent on discovering. In such contexts even the consideration of metrical form can be slanted unfavourably. For instance, it is generally agreed that Keats intended the irregular stanzas of *To Psyche*, with their inserted shorter lines, to produce loosely the effect of a "Pindaric" ode, and it seems to me that this effect is obtained (the unrhyming lines are not much more noticeable than in *Lycidas*). It is only if we become preoccupied with Keats's experiments with the sonnet-form in this ode—experiments which Messrs. Garrod and Ridley have shown to be connected with the evolution of the stanza used in the other odes (a ten-line stanza except in *To Autumn,* which adds an eleventh line)—that we are likely to think that *To Psyche* gives "an uneasy impression of trying to be recurrent and failing." [6] It does

---

[4] An expression borrowed from Robert Bridges.

[5] Pp. 172–73.

[6] Ridley, *Keats' Craftsmanship* (1933), p. 205.

not in fact give such an impression unless we have stopped reading the poem as a poem and are looking at it instead as a stepping-stone to a later metrical perfection.

*       *       *

If we try to forget the other odes and look at *To Psyche* freshly, two immediate impressions seem normal. The first is that the poem opens badly but warms up rapidly after a weak start; the second is that, while the poem is a happy one, its tone is more exactly described if the happiness is thought of as defensive or defiant.

Robert Bridges observed that "the beginning of this ode is not so good," and it needs no special insight to see that Keats could have produced a more arresting opening by deleting his first quatrain with its tasteless echo of *Lycidas* and the displeasing phrase "soft-conched ear" (Elizabethan for the cliché "shell-like ear"). Again, later in the first stanza, the repetition of "grass" in ll. 10 and 15 is clumsy, and the reader is nagged by the distracting survival of the rhymes for a further two lines after the sense has closed in:

A brooklet, scarce espied.

Some of these faults probably came from working over the poem too often and at first, perhaps, too coolly—the price that Keats paid for his "peaceable and healthy spirit" may have been that his "pains" fixed his first stanza against further correction while its elements were still imperfectly combined (the version of the ode in the Pierpont Morgan Library, apparently the earliest that we have, is certainly not a first draft). Here the practical result is that several layers of composition appear to be cobbled together, not inexpertly, but without the ruthlessness of exclusion of otherwise acceptable phrase or rhyme that would have been given by a firm sense of poetic direction. The weakness disappears after the first stanza, which seems to confirm that Keats discovered his real subject in the process of writing—the rise in poetic temperature at the beginning of the third stanza ("O brightest! though too late for antique vows") may announce his full awareness of this discovery. I differ from Bridges about the value of this central section of the ode. He considers that the poem climbs with a steady improvement towards its conclusion and that its middle is only "midway in excellence." I find the first half of the third stanza at least the equal in excellence of the final stanza so admired by Bridges, particularly if his comment is kept in mind that "the imagery is worked up to outface the idea" in the ode's last section. The observation has, of course, a wider and more general application to Keats's poetry—it is simplest to ascribe the "outfacing" to his infatuation with a luxurious Elizabethan diction (as Lady Chatterley remarked to her husband, whom circumstances compelled to prefer Art to Life, "The Elizabethans are so upholstered"). Against the overloaded imagery of the fourth stanza and some weak phrasing earlier, it is fair to set the successful rhyming. *To a Nightingale*, for example, has a bad rhyme in stanza six and forced expressions for the sake of rhyming in the first and last stanzas.

The other immediate impression, that of the ode's defensive happiness, is not easy to pin down, but Keats seems to be rejoicing because of

> . . . having to construct something
> Upon which to rejoice.

There is a defiant assertion that unaided he can put the clock back, that the ode itself proves that his is "a fond believing lyre" in spite of an age

> . . . so far retir'd
> From happy pieties . . . .

Positively, one relates this conviction to the nearness of Fanny Brawne —Keats is in love and for lovers "happy pieties" are still possible.

In any move to go beyond these immediate impressions it is natural to examine carefully the serial letter to George and Georgiana Keats (Letter 123) in which an unrevised version of *To Psyche* is copied out. It cannot, surely, be an accident that this copy of the ode should closely follow Keats's reflections on the world as a "vale of Soul-making." "Do you not see," says Keats, "how necessary a World of Pains and troubles is to school an Intelligence and make it a Soul?" We can hardly fail to link the intelligent "Spark" struggling to become a soul as a result of a "World of Pains and troubles" with the Psyche who achieves apotheosis and happiness after long wanderings and sufferings in search of Cupid. Keats had met the legend in Mrs. Tighe's fantasticated Spenserian version as early as 1817, and he mentions Psyche's woes and her reward in *I stood tip-toe* (ll. 141–50), but the reference to Apuleius in Letter 123 (see below) implies that by 1819 he had looked at a translation of *The Golden Ass*. For Keats the obvious translation was William Adlington's Elizabethan one of 1566, and C. L. Finney has noted verbal parallels between it and the ode.[7] Whether Keats's reflections on soul-making came directly out of his experience of life, and then, remembering that Psyche was the soul, he decided to read Apuleius in Adlington's version, or whether it was a reading of Adlington's account of Psyche's expiatory wanderings that prompted the famous description of soul-making in his let-

---

[7] *The Evolution of Keats's Poetry* (1936), II, 614–15.

ter, cannot be settled and perhaps is not very important. What can
be shown convincingly is that the following passage was in his mind
when he was writing *To Psyche*:

> Thus poore Psyches being left alone, weeping and trembling on the
> toppe of the rocke, was blowne by the gentle aire and of shrilling
> Zephyrus, and caried from the hill with a meek winde, which retained
> her garments up, and by little and little brought her downe into a deepe
> valley, where she was laid in *a bed of most sweet and fragrant flowers.*
> *Thus faire Psyches being sweetly couched among the soft and tender*
> *hearbs, as in a bed of sweet and fragrant floures,* and having qualified
> the thoughts and troubles of her restlesse mind, was now well reposed.
> And when she had refreshed her selfe sufficiently with sleepe, she rose
> with a more quiet and pacified minde, and fortuned to *espy a pleasant*
> *wood invironed with great and mighty trees. Shee espied likewise a*
> *running river as cleare as crystall:* in the midst of the wood well nigh at
> the fall of the river was a princely Edifice, wrought and builded not by
> the art or hand of man.[8]

Professor Finney asks us to set the italicised phrases beside the picture
of Cupid and Psyche in the first stanza of the ode ("couched side by
side / In deepest grass . . . where there ran / A brooklet, scarce espied:
/ 'Mid hush'd, cool-rooted flowers, fragrant-eyed . . . They lay calm-
breathing on the bedded grass"), but these verbal correspondences,
though telling, are not more so than the way in which the landscape
of Keats's fourth stanza reproduces the Apuleius-Adlington setting—
in both descriptions a mountain wall and great trees shut off a flower-
strewn valley containing a retreat or sanctuary. It also weighs a little
with me that Adlington's "she rose with a more quiet and pacified
minde" seems to be crookedly echoed in a passage, already quoted,
from Letter 123 ("to write other things in even a more peaceable and
healthy spirit").

How did Keats first hear of Apuleius? There can be no certainty,
but Lemprière's *Classical Dictionary* (1788) may have been his source.
It is certain that Keats referred to the dictionary—the entry under
"Psyche" is drawn on in his explanation of the ode in Letter 123. In
Lemprière we are told that Psyche is "a nymph whom Cupid married
and conveyed to a place of bliss. . . . The word signifies *the soul,* and
this personification of Psyche, first mentioned by Apuleius, is consequently posterior to the Augustan age, though it is connected with
antient mythology," and again, a little below this, that Cupid's divin-
ity "was universally acknowledged, and vows, prayers, and sacrifices
were daily offered to him." Keats repeats some of the information
for his brother and sister-in-law:

---

[8] Finney's italics. Text from C. Whibley's reprint of the 1639 edition.

You must recollect that Psyche was not embodied as a goddess before the time of Apulieus [*sic*] the Platonist who lived after the A[u]gustan age, and consequently . . . was never worshipped or sacrificed to with any of the ancient fervour—and perhaps never thought of in the old religion—I am more orthodox that [*for* than] to let a heathen Goddess be so neglected.[9]

The similarity of these two accounts is less interesting than the differences between them. It is Keats who calls Apuleius a Platonist, which may strengthen the connection between *To Psyche* and the reflections on soul-making. It is Keats, again, who puts together the two facts of Psyche's late personification and of the daily worship of Cupid in earlier times in order to insist in his letter that the goddess "was never worshipped or sacrificed to with any of the ancient fervour." Apparently this was what struck him most forcibly in Lemprière, so that the dull phrases of the dictionary may be said to govern the form taken by the ode's second stanza with its catalogue of imagined rites and devotions. "This personification . . . is consequently posterior to the Augustan age" is therefore the improbable germ of the apostrophe with which the second stanza opens:

> O latest born and loveliest vision far
> Of all Olympus' faded hierarchy . . . .

Psyche is the "loveliest vision far," lovelier than the Moon or Venus, because she is a love-goddess with an understanding of troubled human experience, because she has known in her own person—as no true Olympian could ever know—suffering and seemingly hopeless longing. She is "loveliest" because she is "latest" (there is much in *Hyperion* and *The Fall of Hyperion* obviously relevant to this identification)—not an early and therefore simple personification of such forces of nature as the wind or the sea, but a late and more sophisticated personification of human nature subjected to an inevitable and cruel process of growing up and growing old. The impatient dismissal of perfectibility ("the nature of the world will not admit of it") with which Keats introduces his sermon on soul-making reveals the passion behind his perception that life is cruel and that to understand it is to be disenchanted. Man, he affirms, is "destined to hardships and disquietude of some kind or other" (Tom had died of tuberculosis only four months earlier). It is this conviction, joined with his awareness of the existential pathos of the human soul (the tragic hero is any man, however fortunate), that makes the celebration of Psyche more than a piece of mythological embroidery; and in Psyche's final apotheosis there may be dimly expressed Keats's longing, which was now almost without hope, for some kind of personal immortality.

9 *Letters*, p. 340.

We need to be aware how closely ideas on the meaning and function of myth were bound up with Keats's attempt to make sense of the human situation. He tells George and Georgiana that his system of soul-making "may have been the Parent of all the more palpable and personal Schemes of Redemption, among the Zoroastrians the Christians and the Hindoos" (Letter 123). That is to say, in these intimate speculations Psyche has for him much the same degree of reality and unreality as "their Christ their Oromanes and their Vishnu." Figures drawn from religious myths—and to Keats Christianity was simply the last of the great mythologies—may be understood sympathetically, he thinks, as personifications of certain kinds of human need or self-knowledge (people "must have the palpable and named Mediator and Saviour"). This is Keats's personal extension of a mode of mythological explanation then a commonplace. It has been conveniently summarised by Hazlitt.

> If we have once enjoyed the cool shade of a tree, and been lulled into a deep repose by the sound of a brook running at its foot, we are sure that wherever we can find a shady stream, we can enjoy the same pleasure again; so that when we imagine these objects, we can easily form a mystic personification of the friendly power that inhabits them, Dryad or Naiad, offering its cool fountain or its tempting shade. Hence the origin of the Grecian mythology.[10]

Keats first met these ideas powerfully in Book IV of Wordsworth's *The Excursion* (see, especially, ll. 847–87), a poem which in one mood he hailed as among the "three things to rejoice at in this Age" (Letter 36, January 10, 1818). Though Wordsworth's influence on Keats's thought has not been fully traced—Book IV of *The Excursion* is quarry for much more in the odes than is generally realized—it is, of course, accepted that Keats expounded Greek myths with a Wordsworthian accent in much of his early poetry, including *Endymion*.

Echoes of Milton's *On the Morning of Christ's Nativity* have been noted in the second stanza of *To Psyche*. De Selincourt, followed by Finney and others, cites the nineteenth stanza of the hymn:

> The Oracles are dumm,
> No voice or hideous humm
>   Runs through the arched roof in words deceiving.
> *Apollo* from his shrine
> Can no more divine,
>   With hollow shreik the steep of *Delphos* leaving

[10] *Lectures on the English Poets,* Lecture V.

> No nightly trance, or breathed spell,
> Inspires the pale-ey'd Priest from the prophetic cell . . .

and finds a parallel in the ode's

> No voice, no lute, no pipe, no incense sweet
> From chain-swung censer teeming;
> No shrine, no grove, no oracle, no heat
> Of pale-mouth'd prophet dreaming.

This, however, does not quite do justice to Keats's memory. Milton's influence is active earlier in stanza two and also extends more subtly to the first half of the ode's third stanza. Thus one line from the twenty-first stanza of the hymn—

> The *Lars,* and *Lemures* moan with midnight plaint . . .

—should be set beside Keats's

> Nor virgin-choir to make delicious moan
> Upon the midnight hours;

and Milton's two preceding lines—

> In consecrated Earth,
> And on the holy Hearth . . .

—lend the force of "consecrated" and "holy," as applied to the elements of earth and fire, to reinforce "haunted" in his twentieth stanza:

> From haunted spring, and dale
> Edg'd with poplar pale,
> The parting Genius is with sighing sent . . .

—and so, I believe, help to inspire Keats's nostalgic

> When holy were the haunted forest boughs,
> Holy the air, the water, and the fire.

It is all much simpler than it sounds in the telling. Only three stanzas of Milton's hymn are involved and their splintering and telescoping in recollection suggest that Keats was not conscious of pastiche.

The chief Miltonic echoes have been recorded, but nobody has stopped to explain why Keats thought of Milton at this point in his poem. Clearly what happened was that "faded" in l. 25 started a train of thought—to which a strong feeling-tone of regret was compulsively attached—about the end of the old Greek world with its "happy pieties" (thought and feeling become explicit in the poem some ten lines later at the beginning of the third stanza). By literary association ideas

of the fading of belief in the Olympian gods and of a lost numinous
nature recalled Milton's description of the departure of the heathen
deities of the Mediterranean world at the birth of Christ. The difference in tone between the two poems could hardly be wider. Milton
writes of the end of heathendom with an almost fierce satisfaction
(though it is certainly possible to detect an undercurrent of tenderness
for the "parting Genius" and "Nimphs in twilight shade" of the classical world). Keats's tone is throughout one of unmixed regret for "the
fond believing lyre," for primitive times with their supposed simplicity and wholeheartedness of feeling. *To Psyche* is now becoming something more than the celebration of a neglected goddess—it projects a
nostalgia for an imagined wholeness of being once possible:

> Le squelette était invisible
> Au temps heureux de l'art païen—

but now, it would seem, impossible (except at lucky moments for the
poet and lover). The nostalgia has also a direct personal application.
Keats's regret for the realm of Flora and old Pan is at the same time
a regret for an earlier phase of his own mental growth before the dis-
enchantment produced by reflection on a darkening experience of the
world. A critic should move as delicately in these matters as if he were
treading on eggshells, but this double reference is unmistakable. It
would be an oversimplification to think of Keats's attitude as "purely
escapist." By the spring of 1819 he was not trying to avoid thoughts of
"Whirlpools and volcanoes"—he had worked his way through at least
to a theoretical acceptance of the value of heartbreaking experience:
what he found it hard to bear was that moments of joy and well-being
should be poisoned by self-consciousness.

> The point at which Man may arrive is as far as the paral[l]el state in
> inanimate nature and no further—For instance suppose a rose to have
> sensation, it blooms on a beautiful morning it enjoys itself—but there
> comes a cold wind, a hot sun—it cannot escape it, it cannot destroy its
> annoyances—they are as native to the world as itself.[11]

Men ought not to be less happy than roses, Keats might have said; and
he believed that those who had—in a phrase from *Endymion*—"culled
Time's sweet first-fruits" had been able to live in the immediate present and were much to be envied. His own power to live in the present,
which lay close to the sources of his poetry, depended for survival, as
he knew, on his skill in preventing the withering of instinctive enjoyment by reflection.

If Keats thought that sun was exchanged for shadow at some necessary stage in the development both of the individual and of human

[11] *Letters*, p. 335.

society as a whole, what was it on the universal plane that corre-
sponded in his view to the over-balance of the reflective power that he
feared in himself? The answer is to be found in *Lamia*—the dangerous
respect given to science (natural philosophy) at the expense of the imagination.

> Do not all charms fly
> At the mere touch of cold philosophy? . . .
> Philosophy will clip an Angel's wings,
> Conquer all mysteries by rule and line,
> Empty the haunted air, and gnomed mine—
> Unweave a rainbow . . . .
>
> (Part I, ll. 229–30, 234–37)

It is known that this passage leans heavily on a paragraph in the first
of Hazlitt's *Lectures on the English Poets*. The paragraph concludes:

> . . . the history of religious and poetical enthusiasms is much the same;
> and both have received a sensible shock from the progress of the experi-
> mental philosophy.

Keats was less simple-minded than Hazlitt, but he accepted this judge-
ment in essence. I do not think he was ever interested in discovering
when this historical change had taken place or begun to take place;
and, in saying so, I do not forget in how many ways he was a child of
the Enlightenment or how mutually antagonistic were some of the
"prose" feelings with which he saluted the March of Mind. But Keats
could not doubt that the poetic experience was valuable, or fail to
suppose that in forgetting Pan men had lost something which they
would not find in the *Transactions* of the Royal Society (the "Fall"
had taken place somewhere between the days of "the fond believing
lyre" and the present). He felt that currents of thought, among the
most reputable and influential of his age, were inimical to the kind of
poetry that he was writing and perhaps to all poetry; and that he
needed to develop his resistance to their influence, and to the influence of the reflective traitor within himself, if he was to remain wholehearted, i.e. keep his capacity for responding poetically to experience.

These ideas and feelings seem relevant to the fourth stanza of *To
Psyche*. Against the background that I have sketched the

> . . . fane
> In some untrodden region of my mind

becomes the "Great Good Place" where the experimental philosophy
rumbles as harmlessly as distant thunder. Keats is constructing a mental landscape for wholehearted enjoyment, and it is fitting that the
scenery should recall the natural setting of the Pan festival in *Endym-*

*ion* and "Time's sweet first-fruits" under the side of Latmos. The similarity of setting can be shown by quotation.

> Far, far around shall those dark-cluster'd trees
>   Fledge the wild-ridged mountains steep by steep;
> And there by zephyrs, streams, and birds, and bees,
>   The moss-lain Dryads shall be lull'd to sleep;
> And in the midst of this wide quietness
> A rosy sanctuary will I dress . . . .
>
> *(To Psyche,* st. 4)

> Upon the sides of Latmos was outspread
> A mighty forest . . .
>
> And it had gloomy shades, sequestered deep,
> Where no man went . . . .
>
>         . . . Paths there were many,
> Winding through palmy fern, and rushes fenny,
> And ivy banks; all leading pleasantly
> To a wide lawn, whence one could only see
> Stems thronging all around between the swell
> Of turf and slanting branches: who could tell
> The freshness of the space of heaven above,
> Edg'd round with dark tree tops? . . .
>
> Full in the middle of this pleasantness
> There stood a marble altar, with a tress
> Of flowers budded newly . . . .
> *(Endymion,* Bk. I, ll. 63–64, 67–68, 79–86, 89–91)

In this "green remote Cockagne," which mixes the scenery of Latmos with the delectable valley in Apuleius, Keats will be able to preserve the visionary poetic experience from marauding analysis—the "shadowy thought" expended for Psyche's delight is the gardener's creative reverie, opposed antithetically to the matter-of-fact operations of scientific logic. And Keats recognizes that keeping one part of the self simple and direct in its receptiveness is a matter intimately linked with the experience of love—the soul's sanctuary is rosy, Milton's "celestial rosie red, love's proper hue." We may note here that both the meeting of Cupid and Psyche in the first stanza and the description of the sanctuary in the fourth stanza have diffuse echoes of Spenser's Garden of Adonis (*Faerie Queene,* Bk. IV, Canto vi) and of the nuptial bower in Eden in *Paradise Lost.*

Since we have to do with a mental landscape, the introduction of Fancy as the gardener is apt enough (though it jars many readers at first). It follows easily as an idea from the Renaissance and neoclassic doctrine that fancy has the power of "retaining, altering and compounding" the images supplied by the senses. The phrase quoted is from No. 411 of *The Spectator,* and in another paper Addison comes very close to thinking of fancy as a gardener when he says that the poet "has the modelling of nature in his own hands" (No. 418). The same doctrine of art's ability to improve on nature may be found earlier in Sidney, Bacon and others; and Puttenham invents his own gardener:

> . . . arte is not only an aide and coadiutor to nature in all her actions, but an alterer of them, and in some sort a surmounter of her skill, so as by meanes of it her owne effects shall appeare more beautifull or straunge or miraculous. . . . the Gardiner by his arte will not onely make an herbe, or flowr, or fruite, come forth in his season without impediment, but will also embellish the same. . . . that nature of her selfe woulde never have done. . . .[12]

Puttenham, Sidney, Bacon and Addison express a stock idea—they are not, of course, in any sense sources of Keats's image, though I suspect that "feign" in

> With all the gardener Fancy e'er could feign

may be a generalized Elizabethan echo. For example, Burton's discussion of Phantasy in *The Anatomy of Melancholy* mentions that it "feigns infinite other unto himselfe" from the images furnished by daily experience. It is an amusing coincidence that Burton should choose "Psyche's palace in Apuleius" as one example of fancy's power. I do not want to make too much of a last remark about "the gardener Fancy," but I think it probable—since Fancy is the true creator of the mental landscape in this stanza—that Keats is glancing at the idea of God as the gardener who designed Eden. Indeed the association seems inevitable if we remember that Adam and Eve cull Time's first-fruits and that *To Psyche* is about a kind of Fall.

If this attempt to understand *To Psyche* is correct in outline, the poem moves through three stages. In the first stage (st. 1, ll. 1–23) Keats sets out to praise Psyche as the neglected goddess whose sufferings and mistakes represent the inevitable conditions of human experience. She has achieved "identity" and lasting happiness. Love is her companion. Keats uses the convention of a sudden vision or waking dream, which comes to him when he is wandering "thoughtlessly," because he had learned to speak in one breath of "the most thoughtless and happiest moments of our Lives" (Letter 183, February 14, 1820), because Spenser's mythological poetry seemed to him a kind of waking

[12] *The Arte of English Poesie,* Lib. III, Ch. xxv.

dream, and because he knew that poetic experience was to be wooed
by opening the mind receptively, not by concentrating its conscious
powers. The vision of Psyche and "the winged boy" in their Eden-like
retreat draws some of its richness, as I have said, from descriptions of
embowered lovers in Spenser and Milton. The tone of this first stanza
is contented, even cool, except for the touch of feeling conveyed by
the repetition "O happy, happy dove," which measures the irksome
distance between the actual world and the happiness that Psyche has
already won.

The second stage of the poem spreads itself over the second and
third stanzas (ll. 24–49). Keats passes easily from the neglect of Psyche
(born as a goddess too late for the fervours of primitive worship) to
the fading and wearing-out of belief in the Olympians, and then to a
nostalgic outpouring of feeling for the magnanimity of life in an age
when all nature was still "holy" (full of the anthropologist's *mana*),
all enjoyment wholehearted, and every herdsman or shepherd the poet
of his own pleasure. The contrast is not with the age of Apuleius, but
with a present which is a twilight for poetic and mythological modes
of thought—the March of Mind has upset the balance of our natures,
making the simple enjoyment of an experience in an "eternal moment" an almost heroic achievement. Keats's regret embraces his own
loss of an earlier innocence. After the first quatrain of the third stanza
we have his defiance of these tendencies and changes in the age and in
himself ("Yet even in these days . . . I see, and sing, by my own eyes
inspired"). At this point the repetition of the catalogue of worship
from the ode's second stanza is a way of suggesting the poet's firmness
or obstinacy. Psyche's worship will not be skimped or abbreviated by
him in an age of unbelief.

The third and final stage of the poem consists of the fourth stanza
(ll. 50–67). Here Keats gets his second wind. The movement introduced by the emphatic

Yes, I will be thy priest . . .

represents an accession of strength. The tread is more measured than
in anything that has gone before, but there is no loss of smoothness or
pace, and the whole stanza, consisting of a single long but quite coher-
ent sentence, develops its momentum quietly at first, then confidently,
and finally with exultation at its climax in the last quatrain. The defiance of the third stanza gives way to confidence as Keats comes to see
how he can worship Psyche (the repetition of "shall" and "will" is ex-
traordinarily positive). Briefly, he will do so by keeping "some untrodden region" of his mind as a safe refuge where Psyche or the soul may
unfold all her powers in a landscape and climate wholly benign and

friendly. The stanza constructs the remoteness and peaceful seclusion
of a valley:

> Far, far around shall those dark-cluster'd trees
> Fledge the wild-ridged mountains steep by steep;
> And there by zephyrs, streams, and birds, and bees,
> The moss-lain Dryads shall be lull'd to sleep.

The succession of pictorial details moves in and down from the dark
mountains and forests to the humming warmth of the valley floor with
its streams and pastoral drowsiness, and the description comes to a focus on Psyche's refuge or shrine:

> And in the midst of this wide quietness
> A rosy sanctuary will I dress . . . .

A complex image, accumulated from these details, is being offered as
the equivalent of a mental state, which may be negatively defined by
what it excludes. Calculation, anxiety and deliberate activity are shut
out. The "wide quietness" of the valley symbolizes a mood in which
the soul will be able to breathe freely, and in which poetry, here defined as "the wreath'd trellis of a working brain" may be coaxed to
put forth its buds and bells and nameless stars. The soul is promised
a rich indolence which will safeguard its natural gift for delight and
restore to wholeness whatever the world beyond the mountains has
broken down. In this luxurious sanctuary, a place made lovely and
inviting with all the resources of a poetic imagination—and these resources are infinite, for Fancy

> . . . breeding flowers, will never breed the same . . .

—Psyche will be disposed to welcome the visits of love (whose "soft
delight" was still for Keats the soul's "chief intensity"). Perhaps the
final implications are that wholeheartedness can never be lost while
Psyche is willing to welcome love in at her casement, and, less directly,
that love, poetry and indolence are the natural medicines of the soul
against the living death it must expect from "cold philosophy."

# Keats's *Ode to a Nightingale*

## *by Richard Harter Fogle*

The *Nightingale* ode has been judiciously dealt with from inside the tradition of Keats scholarship by such experts as Sir Sidney Colvin, Ernest de Sélincourt, Douglas Bush, and H. W. Garrod. Recent reinterpretations by Brooks and Warren, by Thomas and Brown, by Allen Tate, F. R. Leavis, Marshall McLuhan, G. Wilson Knight, Albert Guérard, Jr., and others, have brought the *Ode* into contact with current critical theories. In following them here I can, I believe, be most useful by steering something of a middle course between the modern and traditional: with, however, an unusual emphasis upon general English Romanticism. My explication, then, will consider the *Ode to a Nightingale* as a Romantic poem, and will venture some exposition of its Romantic principles. I shall also try to bear in mind the implications of recent criticism.

The *Nightingale* is a Romantic poem of the family of *Kubla Khan* and *The Eve of St. Agnes* in that it describes a choice and rare experience, intentionally remote from the commonplace. Nowadays we sometimes underrate the skill required for this sort of thing. The masters of Romantic magic were aware that ecstasy, for example, is not adequately projected by crying, "I am ecstatic!" Keats gets his effects in the *Nightingale* by framing the consummate moment in oppositions, by consciously emphasizing its brevity; he sets off his ideal by the contrast of the actual. The principal stress of the poem is a struggle between ideal and actual: inclusive terms which, however, contain more particular antitheses of pleasure and pain, of imagination and commonsense reason, of fullness and privation, of permanence and change, of nature and the human, of art and life, freedom and bondage, waking and dream. These terms are of course only expedients; they are products of "that false secondary power which multiplies distinctions," and I fear might easily be multiplied still further. I defend them as the best I am able to frame, and as necessary for analysis.

The drugged, dull pain in lines 1–4 is a frame and a contrast for the poignant pleasure of the climax; at the same time, it is inseparable

"*Keats's* Ode to a Nightingale" *by Richard Harter Fogle. Reprinted by permission of the Modern Language Association from* PMLA, LXVIII (1953), 211–22.

from it. "Extremes meet," as Coleridge was fond of saying, and as Keats also has said elsewhere in *A Song of Opposites* and the *Ode on Melancholy*. They meet because they *are* extremes, as very hot and cold water are alike to the touch—their extremity is their affinity— and because of a Romantic prepossession to unity of experience, which in Keats was a matter of temperament as well as of conviction. Both pleasure and pain are deliberately heightened, and meet in a common intensity. The pain is the natural sequel of "too much happiness," the systole to the diastole of joy.

> 'Tis not through envy of thy happy lot,
> But being too happy in thine happiness . . . .

Despite this disavowal of envy, perhaps the envy is about the same as being "too happy." The felicity which is permanent in the nightingale is transient and therefore excessive in the poet. It is too heavy a burden to be borne more than briefly, and dangerous in its transience. Its attractions make everyday living ugly by contrast. Cleanth Brooks has defined as the theme of the poem "the following paradox: the world of the imagination offers a release from the painful world of actuality, yet at the same time it renders the world of actuality more painful by contrast." [1] Allen Tate has called the *Nightingale* "an emblem of one limit of our experience: the impossibility of synthesizing, in the order of experience, the antinomy of the ideal and the real." [2] Both statements strike into the crucial dilemma of the Romantic imagination, a basic *donnée* of the Romantic poet which he may turn to his advantage or his bane as he is able to cope with it. Good Romantic poems, like *Kubla Khan* and the *Nightingale,* define this dilemma, dramatize it, and transform it to a source of strength. Such poetry accepts the risk to get at the value, in full awareness of the issues. To affirm either that the difficulty itself is avoidable, or that it could be definitively solved by a properly framed discourse, would be to talk of something other than poetry.

The theme of stanza 2 is plenitude. The ideal lies in fullness. The nightingale sings "in full-throated ease," the longed-for beaker is "full of the warm South, / Full of the true, the blushful Hippocrene." This fullness contrasts with the sad satiety of stanza 3, "Where but to think is to be full of sorrow"; it is modulated in the "embalmed darkness" of stanza 5, in richness of sensuous texture; and it ends in stanza 6 in a climactic fullness of song:

[1] *Modern Poetry and the Tradition* (Chapel Hill: Univ. of North Carolina Press, 1939), p. 31.
[2] "A Reading of Keats," *On the Limits of Poetry* (New York: Swallow Press, 1948), p. 177.

> While thou art pouring forth thy soul abroad
> In such an ecstasy!

The fabric of stanza 2 is too fine for common wear, a happiness too great, a conjunction of circumstances impossibly appropriate. The draught of vintage has been "Cooled *a long age* in the *deep-delved* earth," the quite un-Miltonic fount of the Muses is "the *true,* the *blushful* Hippocrene," and the beaker is brim-full, with "purple-stained mouth." Such concentration of effect is probably what Keats had in mind when he advised Shelley to "load every rift with ore." Here it is used to image a Golden Age, before Jove reigned, of fullness, gusto, ease, and freedom. To achieve this ideal, however, the imagination builds upon the finite actual. The passage is deliberately pure and quintessential—the ore has been refined—and in its purity delicately defiant and mirthful. Such writing is a Romantic equivalent of metaphysical wit. It differs from the metaphysical mode in its more thorough subordination to the total meaning.

The draught of vintage, itself an instrument of imagination, symbolizes an imaginative escape from actuality. The longing to "fade away into the forest dim" is in order to avoid another kind of fading away, the melancholy dissolutions of change and physical decay. The world of stanza 3 is the antitype of the golden world of 2: for ease is substituted "the weariness, the fever, and the fret," for plenitude "a few, sad, last grey hairs." It is a world of privation, "Where youth grows pale, and spectre-thin, and dies."

In his judicial reading of the *Ode to a Nightingale* Mr. Allen Tate finds little to say for this stanza. It is bad eighteenth-century personification, without on the one hand Pope's precision, or the energy of Blake on the other. "It gives us," says Mr. Tate, ". . . a 'picture' of common reality, in which the life of man is all mutability and frustration. But here if anywhere in the poem the necessity to dramatize time or the pressure of actuality, is paramount. *Keats has no language of his own for this realm of experience*" (p. 174). Keats's mode is pictorial, and this mode "allows him to present the thesis of his dilemma, the ideality of the nightingale symbol, but not the antithesis, the world of common experience, which is the substance of stanza three. . . . The climax contains a little less than the full situation; it reaches us a little too simplified" (p. 176).

My dissent can be summarized in the counter-assertion that, with certain inevitable reservations, the privation is as vividly realized as is the ideal plenitude. The personifications of age, youth, beauty, and love are vitalized by their contexts; they are comparable to "Veiled Melancholy" in "her sovran shrine" in the *Ode on Melancholy,* and the personifications of *To Autumn.* The particulars transform the abstractions, which are themselves explicable as necessary economies in

a broadly typical account. (Any sort of detailed and documented realism would be unthinkable.) Time and the pressure of actuality, Mr.
Tate to the contrary, are dramatized in parellelism, repetition, and
progression. "The weariness, the fever, and the fret"; "a few, sad, last
grey hairs"; "grows pale, and spectre-thin, and dies"; here is the process of tedium, time, and decay; here is the very movement of the meaning. The fourfold repetition of "Where" is a further reinforcement,
with its rhetorical suggestion of rising emotion to counterbalance the
falling series of time. The stanza, one may well assert, has an intensity
equal to its antithesis of the imaginative ideal, as Douglas Bush has
remarked in his persuasive argument that the real theme of Keats's
six great odes is the sadness of mutability.[3] It has also, what Professor
Bush failed to point out, an energy of thought and a complex suavity
which is best indicated in the last two lines—an effect in which personification plays a considerable part.

One grows uncomfortably aware of the limits of explication upon
such an issue. I cannot say what shadows of Tom Keats and Fanny
Brawne may haunt my reading of stanza 3, nor what reverberations
from that old-fashioned doctrine of sincerity. One is left, at any rate,
with a feeling that objective analysis goes only halfway—an avowal
the humility of which is perhaps damaged by the fact that I wish to
hit Mr. Tate with it more than myself. Assuming that Keats is a pictorial poet, he finds stanza 3 inadequately pictorial. Here he is push-
ing a metaphor too far. The *Nightingale* does not seem a notably pictorial poem; in it the associations of objects are much more important
than their outlines.

The crucial issue, however, is the conception of unity implied by
Mr. Tate's criticism. What can properly be asked of a poem? The first
consideration in the *Nightingale* ode is the imaginative experience of
the ideal. Different elements come into the picture, but there is at
bottom one emphasis only. The objection to stanza 3 comes from very
interesting assumptions about the nature of poetic unity, wholeness,
and the reconciliation of opposites, which should be examined.

According to these assumptions unity is less important than wholeness, which in turn might be defined as an ideal reconciliation of all
possible opposites. I argue against them that no poem is whole in this
sense, or finally in any but its own terms. No poem contains all modes
of experience, or even two experiences or ideas projected with equal
force. The reconciliation of equal opposites is a theoretical, not an
actual process; it would be colorless, odorless, tasteless, faceless. All
logical opposites stand to each other in a dual relationship. They are
first conceived as equals in that they are opposed; but they then ar-

[3] *Mythology and the Romantic Tradition in English Poetry* (Cambridge, Mass.:
Harvard Univ. Press, 1937), p. 107.

range themselves in varying relations of inequality. Imagination can be reconciled to reason as the whole of which reason is a part; or the relation may be one of predominance, in which some elements of the weaker opposite are sacrificed to bring it into line—as a conservative will argue that he has incorporated the best features of progressivism into his conservative system. Opposites can be reconciled through related qualities of feeling, or simply by having common attributes. In a loose sense they may be said to be reconciled through the fact that they co-exist, as in the Romantic assumption that reality is One. The concept of the reconciliation of opposites, then, covers many processes, none of which corresponds precisely with the theoretical ideal. And none of these processes can be dismissed as in itself incomplete or dishonest.

If a poem, then, is thought of as a logical argument (which is to use an imperfect metaphor), the poet is under no obligation to do literal justice to both sides of the question, which would in any event be impossible. He does enough if he makes his argument interesting. If he also shows an awareness of other opinions, so much the better. If he seems crucially engaged with his problem we permit him to be a little unceremonious. In the *Nightingale* Keats is both interesting and as well-mannered as a man need be who is expressing his convictions. He is affirming the value of the ideal, and this is the primary fact. He is also paying due tribute to the power of the actual, and this is an important but secondary consideration. The stress of the poem lies in the conflict of value and power. Keats is at once agonized and amused at the inescapable discrepancy between them. He reconciles them by a prior imaginative acceptance of the unity of experience, by means of which he invests them with a common extremity and intensity of feeling. He need not give equal attention to both, for the actual can take care of itself; it is the frail ideal which requires bolstering.

The manner of Keats's reconciliation of opposites appears in stanza 4:

> Not charioted by Bacchus and his pards,
> But on the viewless wings of Poesy . . . .

This rejection is only ostensible. Like Coleridge, and as W. H. Auden has lately remarked about the Romantics in general, Keats prefers "both . . . and" to "either . . . or." The "draught of vintage" is not cancelled by, but combined with the vision in the forest, which deepens rather than discards the suggestions of "Flora and the country green." The intuitive speed of imagination is dramatized by "Already with thee!" The forest scene is Romantically picturesque without being really pictorial: one does not visualize it, but its composition is describable in visual metaphor. Its unity is a matter of blending, with objects softened and distanced by the veil of darkness, which itself shades off into moonlight filtered through forest leaves. The moonlight, a symbol of imagination, intermingling with darkness evokes the enchantment of mystery, the wondrous secret just out of reach. After thus using suggestion Keats goes on to specification, much as he has done with "Bacchus and his pards." The imagery is particular and sensuous, but not highly visual. Hawthorn, eglantine, violets, and musk rose are important chiefly for their pastoral associations.

In the total effect sensations are blended in a soft and complex unity. Odor merges with touch and kinesthetic strain in "what soft incense hangs upon the boughs." "The grass, the thicket, and the fruit tree wild" have tactual and plastic qualities. The "fast fading violets" are invested with organic sensation through empathy by being "covered up in leaves," and the associations of the musk rose include taste and sound. As in stanza 2 the theme is fullness, but with an added poignance and complexity from the introduction of darkness and death. The generous fertility of Nature is inseparable from the grave, the height demands its complement in depth, and intensest life turns imperceptibly to its opposite.

The death theme, however, may easily be made too much of. The embalmed darkness and the fast fading violets certainly suggest it, but the imaginative escape of stanza 4 is less into death (or the womb) than into an ideal nature. The death of stanza 5 is, indeed, a reasonable inference from the experience of the forest. As freedom, ease, intensity, plenitude, and consummation the two are one. Death is easeful and rich, it is associated with the nightingale's song in lavishness of giving. "To cease upon the midnight" is in one respect the same as "pouring forth thy soul abroad." In each is an outpouring, and a release from the prisoning self. This imaginative acceptance of death is not, however, unreserved. "I have been *half* in love with easeful Death" and "Now more than ever seems it rich to die" are measured statements. The acceptance, in fact, includes the reservation, since it is an acceptance of the limits as well as the freedoms of this death:

> Still wouldst thou sing, and I have ears in vain—
> To thy high requiem become a sod.

Momentarily death has identified Keats with the nightingale, but only momentarily. Its meaning shifts from the most heightened consciousness to blank oblivion, and what seemed pure spirit is sheer inert mass.

In another swift transition the death theme turns to a basis for the immortality of the nightingale: a shift which restresses both the identification and the withdrawal from the identification. We are probably no longer greatly troubled by the objection seen by Robert Bridges, that the bird is obviously *not* immortal.[4]

H. W. Garrod has remarked that the nightingale commences as a particular bird, but is imaginatively transformed to a myth in such phrases as "light-winged Dryad of the trees."[5] The objection has also been met by the suggestion that Keats is thinking of the species, not the individual nightingale. Both of these solutions seem provisionally true; a little further on I wish to comment on the mortal-immortal difficulty as it is peculiar to Keats's imagination. In stanza 7, at any rate, the bird is a universal and undying voice: the voice of nature, of imaginative sympathy, and therefore of an ideal Romantic poetry, infinitely powerful and profuse (compare the "profuse strains of unpremeditated art" of Shelley's *Skylark,* and the "music loud and long" of *Kubla Khan*). As sympathy it resolves all differences into the main fact of what Hawthorne has called the magnetic chain of humanity. It speaks to high and low; it comforts the human homesickness of Ruth and frees her from bitter isolation; and equally it opens the casements of the remote and magical. Lines 65–70 perhaps contain the two kinds of Romanticism which Coleridge differentiated in Chapter xiv of *Biographia Literaria*: but the domestic and the exotic varieties are linked by their common purpose of fusing the usual with the strange. Ruth is distanced and framed by time and rich association, but in relation to the magic casements she is homely and familiar.

These magic casements are the apex and the climax of the imaginative experience. They are deliberately towering and frail, dramatizing the value, the gallantry, and the precariousness of the Romantic imagination at its height. They are connected with the actual by defying it, by their affirmation that what the mind can imagine is beauty and truth, an experience to be prized all the more for its brevity. The different senses of "forlorn," upon which Mr. Brooks has acutely commented (p. 31), relate the passage to Ruth as well as to the final stanza, which returns to common earth. Ruth is forlorn in her loneliness. The faery lands are pleasurably forlorn in a remoteness which is really the condition of their value. "Forlorn" is like a bell which tolls the death of the imagination.

Stanza 8, despite the suddenness of the transition, is nevertheless a soft and quiet withdrawal from the heights. "The fancy cannot cheat so well / As she is famed to do" is not a rejection of imagination, but part of the total experience. The diction is unobtrusively lowered, to give an effect of half-humorous ruefulness. The inner movement of the

---

[4] Introd., *Poems of John Keats,* ed. G. Thorn Drury (New York: E. P. Dutton and Co., n.d.), p. lxiv.

[5] *Keats* (Oxford: Clarendon Press, 1926), pp. 113–14.

conclusion is objectified in the gradual fading of the song, "Past the near meadows, over the still stream, / Up the hillside," in a perfect fusion of outward setting with mental experience. I am unable to see deep significance in the fact that the bird is now "buried deep / In the next valley-glade," but it would seem that it works like Wordsworth's

> But there's a tree, of many, one,
> A single field which I have looked upon,
> Both of them speak of something that is gone,

by emphasizing a difference in sameness. The line recalls the "embalmed darkness" of the forest dim, and thus realizes the gulf between the earlier participation and the final withdrawal.

> Was it a vision, or a waking dream?
> Fled is that music:—do I wake or sleep?

These questions are objective in that they portray rather than abstract from Keats's state of mind. Like the beginning of the poem they suggest a prostrating reaction to an experience too powerful to be mastered, while as questions they also express an attempt to control and to understand it. Intellectually they raise a vital issue of Romanticism, which might be underlined by remembering that Keats's original draft ran, "Was it a vision *real* or waking dream?" [6] It is the problem of the truth of imagination, which adds a further tension to the various stresses of actual and ideal. "I am certain," wrote Keats, "of nothing but of the holiness of the heart's affections, and the truth of imagination. What the imagination seizes as beauty must be truth." [7] Which was the dream, and which the reality? Which was the true, the peak or the plain, the rare or the commonplace, the ideal of permanence or the fact of change?

The answer concerns our problem of the reconciliation of opposites. The imaginative ideal is in a sense more true because it is more valuable, and the *Ode to a Nightingale* celebrates the poetic imagination. As it opposes the ideal to the actual, imagination against commonsense reason, imagination and ideal still predominate. They stand to their opposites as high against low, apex against base, action against reaction. Ideal and actual meet only as extremes, joined in the circle of experience. But the full power of the poem comes from adding the deadly question, is not the worse the true, the better the illusion? Should we not change the meaning of truth?

[6] See Sir Sidney Colvin, "A Morning's Walk in a Hampstead Garden," in *The John Keats Memorial Volume* (London: John Lane, 1921), p. 73.

[7] *The Letters of John Keats*, ed. M. B. Forman (London: Oxford Univ. Press, 1947), p. 67. Punctuation and capitals are altered from Forman's text.

The *Ode to a Nightingale* contains the highest, the fullest, the most intense, the most valuable mental experience which Keats can imagine. This is its center, this the basis of its unity. Within this unity, however, is a complex of feeling and thought which moves in alternate swellings and subsidences, a series of waves, each with its attendant trough. These waves are not of equal height; they rise gradually to a climax in stanza 7, and the rise subsides in the conclusion. Herbert Marshall McLuhan has suggested the musical organization of the fugue to define the structures of Keats's odes.[8] Most ambitious Romantic poems of inner experience, indeed, offer wide variety of mood, with sudden and dramatic transitions. The *Ode on Intimations of Immortality*, with its organ-like swellings and sinkings, and its abrupt and effective changes of direction, is similar to the *Nightingale* in organization. Both make central affirmations, and both make these affirmations interesting by providing a controlled complexity of movement based upon a crucial suspense. Keats concludes with a question and Wordsworth with an answer, of course, but then Wordsworth knew more answers than Keats.

I have repeatedly made use of the metaphors of wholeness and intensity in this essay. In explication they are radically metaphors, I believe, rather than complete concepts. The theory of wholeness earlier imputed to Mr. Tate is a characteristically modern idea, equivalent to the metaphysical wit described by Eliot, the inclusive poetry of Richards, the ironic poetry of Brooks and Warren, and the modern poetry of knowledge adumbrated by John Crowe Ransom in *The World's Body*, which is not the poetry of children, nor of the heart's desire, but of the fallen mind, "since ours too are fallen." Such poetry is to be armed at all points, invulnerable to irony. Nothing can be objected to it, for it has foreseen all objections. It is a poetry of wholeness in that it has synthesized all conceivable arguments and attitudes. It follows that its conception of synthesis emphasizes the number and the diversity of the elements to be synthesized, and gives correspondingly less attention to the synthesizing agent. A poem constructed on this theory would emphasize difficulties and contradictions, discords and roughness, and only on inspection should its unity emerge, ideally the more satisfying because it has been struggled for.

Keats's notion of wholeness has the same elements as the modern, but with a different order and emphasis. "The excellence of every art is its intensity, capable of making all disagreeables evaporate, from their being in close relationship with Beauty and Truth." [9] Here the agent of synthesis comes first, the unity and the harmony, not the com-

---

[8] "Aesthetic Pattern in Keats's Odes," *Univ. of Toronto Quart.*, XII (1943), 167–68.
[9] *Letters of Keats*, p. 71.

plexity and the discordance. The "disagreeables" must be attended to, but Keats is confident that they can be "evaporated" in intensity. The difference in emphasis might be illustrated in Tate's comments on Longinus' famous account of Sappho's ode. In Longinus Mr. Tate sees an early exponent of the reconciliation of opposites, who is using wholeness and complexity as his criteria of excellence.[10] A Romantic, however, would probably settle first upon the passion which has unified the complexity, and would then interest himself in Longinus' remarks about the principle of selection in the poem. Sappho does not give everything, but only a selected part of the whole. The ode is an essence, not an imitation of reality. The details are chosen for the greatest intensity of concentration, with the irrelevant and trivial excluded.

Intense concentration of effect in Keats, the loading every rift with ore, is a way of obtaining profusion, as the *Nightingale* itself demonstrates. F. R. Leavis has said that "One remembers the poem both as recording, and as being for the reader, an indulgence." [11] I find Mr. Leavis too austere, but he points out a quality which Keats plainly sought for. His profusion and prodigality is, however, modified by a principle of sobriety. He has recorded both the profusion and its attendant restraint:

1st. I think poetry should surprise by a fine excess, and not by singularity; it should strike the reader as a wording of his own highest thoughts, and appear almost as a remembrance.

2nd. Its touches of beauty should never be halfway, thereby making the reader breathless, instead of content. The rise, the progress, the setting of Imagery should, like the sun, come natural to him, shine over him, and set soberly, although in magnificence, leaving him in the luxury of twilight. . . .

Another axiom—That if poetry comes not as naturally as the leaves to a tree, it had better not come at all.[12]

This passage can be taken, I think, to represent the artistic purposes of the *Nightingale*. Wholeness, intensity, and naturalness are its appropriate standards. Nature is, indeed, the real norm—the physical face of nature, nature as it appears to the Romantic imagination—and wholeness and intensity are attributes of nature, as are freedom, ease, spontaneity, harmony, and sobriety. Imagined as the Golden Age of Flora and the country green, and more fully as the forest of the

[10] "Longinus," in *Lectures in Criticism* (New York: Pantheon Books, 1949), pp. 61–62.
[11] *Revaluation* (London: Chatto and Windus, 1936), p. 244.
[12] *Letters of Keats*, p. 108. Punctuation and capitals altered.

nightingale, it becomes first the bird, the voice of nature; then the ideal poet; and finally the ideal itself. This nature is the antithesis of the privative actual in stanza 3.

The nature of the *Nightingale* is particular, since it conforms to its dramatic situation. The rich darkness of the forest is peculiar to the poem, not literally entire and universal. The poet uses his *donnée*, and no extension of his symbols will transcend its limits. Given his particular and concrete nature, Keats infers from it peace, fulfillment, and ideal freedom. His apprehension of nature is characteristically Romantic but peculiarly his own in its sensuous immediacy. While he feels the Romantic impulsion toward an overarching and ideal unity, in him the sensuous real is inseparable from its ideal opposite. It is as if for Keats the primary and secondary imaginations of Coleridge were one, and the process of "dissolving, diffusing, dissipating, in order to recreate" unnecessary to him. To his apprehension physical nature is immediately absolute and permanent. In the *Nightingale*, as in *To Autumn*, he arrests change in mid-motion by contemplation apotheosized, which fixes the temporal object within a timeless frame. And thus the immortality of the nightingale; it is a question of focus. Nature is always dying but always alive, forever changing but always the same. With the nightingale Keats fixes his imagination upon sameness and life.

The standard of nature involves effects of spontaneity and artlessness which sometimes confuse us into suspecting that the poet is confusing his art with reality. The Romantics have laid themselves open to this misconstruction, but it is nevertheless a great mistake to take their artistic imitations for experience in the raw. The *Nightingale* imitates spontaneity without being spontaneous. Its opening lines, for example, are calculated to disarm judgment by a show of unrehearsed feeling. These lines are, however, a classic instance of Keats's technique. The repeated suggestions in "as though of hemlock I had drunk," "emptied some dull opiate to the drains," and "Lethe-wards had sunk," with their undersong of assonance, are obviously more than coincidental.

The transitional links of the poem are also at first sight spontaneous and merely associational. They are too invariably happy, however, to be literally unpremeditated. H. W. Garrod has asserted that the transitions of the *Nightingale* are governed by Keats's intoxication with his own words. ". . . the infection of his own accidents of style, if I may so call them, compels the direction of thought; the rhythm and words together determine the stanza which comes next. . . ." [13] One wonders what or who determines the rhythm and words. More recently

[13] *Keats*, p. 111.

Albert Guérard, Jr., viewing the *Nightingale* as a poem which consummately expresses the universal impulse toward submersion of consciousness, has said that this impulse is a "longing not for art but a free reverie of any kind. The form of the poem is that of progression by association, so that the movement of feeling is at the mercy of words evoked by chance, such words as *fade* and *forlorn*, the very word which like a bell tolls the dreamer back to his sole self." [14] This passage occurs in an interesting and a favorable account of the poem. Mr. Guérard, like Mr. Garrod, admires Keats. Nevertheless, "longing not for art but a free reverie of any kind," and "the movement of the feeling is at the mercy of words evoked by chance" constitute damaging charges, indicting the Ode for bad art and low-grade mental activity. Such charges against Romantic poems have become rather frequent since Babbitt reigned. A Romantic critic still has trouble answering them, however, because their assumptions are strange to him. One is always dismayed to find what he had happily taken for a virtue suddenly and persuasively attacked as one of the lower forms of vice.

I will nevertheless venture some suggestions on the specific problem of associational transitions like "fade away" and "forlorn." To adopt Mr. McLuhan's musical analogy, they are motifs woven into a varied musical pattern. Dramatically they are important in objectifying the theme in a word, revealing instantaneously the central stress of the poem. They work like Wordsworth's tree, which focusses the problem of his ode, "Where is it now, the glory and the dream?" in a single concrete image. So "fade away" and "forlorn" dramatize sharply the two states of mind in the poem. Why they should be said to control the movement of the feeling is not clear to me; they appear only to *indicate* the movement, as patches of foam on the tops of the swells.

It is easy to make nonsense of the Romantic aesthetic of nature by noticing only its major term, and omitting its elaborate qualifications. Coleridge gives its true emphasis, I think, in describing poetic imagination as the power which "while it blends and harmonizes the natural and the artificial, still subordinates art to nature, the manner to the matter; and our admiration of the poet to our sympathy with the poetry." [15] The natural must be blended with the artificial; art is to be subordinated, not extinguished. In this context art is to be understood as the appearance of art, as it strikes the eye of the beholder; Coleridge is not establishing a quota on the art which can actually go into the poem.

[14] "Prometheus and the Aeolian Lyre," *Yale Review*, XXXIII (1944), 495.
[15] *Biographia Literaria*, Ch. xiv.

# The *Ode to a Nightingale*

## *by* *Cleanth Brooks and Robert Penn Warren*

In this poem the world of mankind and the world of the nightingale stand over against each other. The listener in the human world responds to the song of the nightingale and, caught up into reverie, yearns to find his way into the world in which the bird sings "of summer in full-throated ease." What the world of the nightingale means to the listener is conveyed in great part through the imagery of the poem. It is a world of richness and vitality, of deep sensuousness, of natural beauty and fertility, but it is not grossly sensuous; it appeals to the imagination and has its own ideality.

Invoking the help of wine and then of poetry, the speaker aspires to attain the nightingale's felicity. But the very description of the wine makes it not so much a passport to the world of the nightingale as a vintage belonging to that world. Indeed the transition from wine to poetry is perfectly smooth, for the wine as realized in the second stanza turns into poetry—a poetic evocation of the spirit of wine.

The images are lovingly elaborated, and the slowed movement of the images resembles the slowed movement of meditative trance or reverie. The reverie carries the listener deep into the "embalmèd darkness" out of which the bird is singing and deep into a communion in which he can make his peace even with death. But the meditative trance cannot last. With the very first word of the eighth stanza, the reverie is broken. The word "forlorn" occurs to the listener as the adjective describing the remote and magical world evoked by the nightingale's song—"in faery lands forlorn." But the listener suddenly realizes that *forlorn* applies only too accurately to himself. The effect is that of an abrupt stumbling. With the new and chilling meaning of "forlorn," the song of the nightingale itself alters: what had a moment before been an ecstatic "high requiem" becomes a "plaintive anthem."

The song becomes fainter: what had had power to make the sorrowing man "fade . . . away" from a harsh and bitter world, now itself "fades" (line 75) and the speaker is left alone in the silence.

*Ode to a Nightingale* is a very rich poem. It contains some complications which we must not gloss over if we are to appreciate the depth and significance of the issues engaged. One of these complications has to do with the close connection between pleasure and pain; another, with that between life and death.

The song of the nightingale has a curious double effect. It makes the listener's heart "ache," but makes it ache, as he is to say in line 6, from "being too happy in thine happiness." The song also acts as an opiate, making the listener feel drowsy and benumbed. Opiates are used to deaden pain, and in a sense the song of the bird does give the man momentary surcease from his unhappiness, oppressed as he is with the "weariness, the fever, and the fret" of the world of humanity.

The student will have to decide whether there is confusion here in this first stanza or an admirable condensation. The initial effect of a heavy opiate, though it leads to an escape from pain in drowsy forgetfulness—"Lethe-wards"—may indeed be painfully numbing. (He who drank of the waters of the river Lethe forgot the sadness of life.) The drowsiness also looks forward to the sense of tranced reverie which is the mood of most of the poem. In that mood the listener does try very hard to immerse himself in the happiness of the bird, projecting himself imaginatively into the world that the bird seems to inhabit.

With the listener's attempt to find his way into the world of the nightingale, we encounter the second complication, that in which death and life change relationship. The nightingale's song makes him yearn to escape from a world overshadowed by death—"where youth grows pale . . . and dies," "Where but to think is to be full of sorrow." Yet when he has approached closest to the nightingale's world, the highest rapture that he can conceive of is to die—"To cease upon the midnight with no pain." [1] The world of the nightingale is, as we shall see, not a world untouched by death—natural processes involve death—but one in which death is not a negative and blighting thing. But at this point the most useful thing to ask ourselves is, "What is it that bars the speaker from entering the world of the nightingale?" He tells us himself: it is the "dull brain" that "perplexes and retards." The opiate, the draught of vintage for which he had earlier called, and the free play of the imagination ("the viewless wings of Poesy")—all have this in common: they release one from the tyranny of the "dull brain."

---

[1] It would be a superficial reading that would make the issue between a painless and an agonizing death. The speaker is saying much more than that he would like to die if he could only be sure that his death would be without pain.

The brain insists upon clarity and logical order; it is an order that must be "dissolved" if the speaker is to escape into, and merge himself with, the richer world for which he longs.

But the word which the speaker uses to describe this process is "fade." His entry into this world of the nightingale is a fading into the rich darkness out of which the nightingale sings. We associate darkness with death, but this darkness is instinct with the most intense life. How is the darkness stressed—and thus defined? The nightingale sings in a plot of "shadows numberless" (line 9); the speaker would leave the world "unseen" (line 19) and join the bird in "the forest dim" (line 20); he would "fade far away"—would "dissolve" (line 21); and when he feels that he is actually with the nightingale, he is in a place of "verdurous glooms" (line 40).

The stress upon a darkness in which clear relations are blotted out continues through the fifth stanza. Having attained to the bird's dark covert, he "cannot see." Though the passage abounds in sensuous detail and appeals so powerfully to all the senses, most of the images of sight are *fancied* by the speaker. He does not actually see the Queen-Moon or the stars. He "guess[es]" at what flowers are at his feet. He has found his way into a warm "embalmèd darkness." The last adjective means primarily "filled with incense," "sweet with balm," but it must also have suggested death—in Keats's day as well as in ours. In finding his way imaginatively into the dark covert, the speaker has approached death. He has wished to fade far away, "dissolve, and quite forget"; but the final dissolution and the ultimate forgetting is death. True, death here is apprehended in a quite different fashion from the death depicted in the third stanza. Here the balm is the natural perfume of growing flowers and the gloom is "verdurous," with suggestions of rich organic growth. But the fading has been complete—he is completely encompassed with darkness.

It is worth remarking that Keats has described the flowery covert with full honesty. If his primary emphasis is on fertility and growth, he accepts the fact that death and change have their place here too: the violets, for instance, are thought of as "fast-fading." But the atmosphere of this world of nature is very different from that of the human world haunted by death, where "men sit and hear each other groan." The world of nature is a world of cyclic change (the "seasonable month," "the coming musk-rose") and consequently can seem fresh and immortal, like the bird whose song seems to be its spirit.

Let us suggest that the poem is not only about man's world as contrasted with the world of nature, or death and deathlessness, but also about alienation and wholeness. It is man's necessary alienation from nature that invests death with its special horror. To "dissolve"—to "fade"—into the warm darkness is to merge into the eternal pattern of nature. In such a communion, death itself becomes something positive—a flowering, a fulfillment.[2]

The bird lacks man's self-consciousness. It is not alienated from nature, but wholly merged in nature. Such considerations suggest the sense in which the nightingale is "immortal." The bird shares in the immortality of nature which, harmonious with itself, remains, through all its myriad changes, unwearied and beautiful. We need not suppose that the speaker, even in his tranced reverie, thinks of this bird—this particular biological mechanism of flesh and bone and feathers—as deathless, any more than he thinks of the "fast-fading violets" and the "coming musk-rose" as unwithering. Keats makes perfectly clear the sense in which the nightingale is immortal: it is in harmony with its world—not, as man is, in competition with his ("No hungry generations tread thee down," line 62); and the bird cannot conceive of its separation from the world which it expresses and of which it is a part ("Thou wast not born for death," line 61). Man knows that he was born to die, knows "The weariness, the fever, and the fret" of the world of mortality, knows in short "What thou among the leaves hast never known" (line 22); and this knowledge overshadows man's life and all his songs.

Such knowledge overshadows the Ode and gives it its special poignancy. With the word "forlorn," the speaker's attempt to enter the world of the nightingale collapses. The music which almost succeeded in making him "fade far away" now itself "fades / Past the near meadows" (lines 75–76) and in a moment is "buried deep / In the next valley-glades" (lines 77–78). The word "buried" conveys in this context a view of death very different from that conjured up by "embalmèd darkness" in the fifth stanza. The poem has come full circle. The speaker, like the knight in Keats's *La Belle Dame sans Merci,* is left alone "On the cold hill's side."

[2] Keats has stressed this association very cunningly in the sixth stanza. The men of the ancient world thought that at death a man breathed out his soul with his last breath. In the seventh stanza, the nightingale is "pouring forth" its "soul"; and at this high moment, the man who is listening in the darkness thinks it would be "rich to die." The most intense expression of life (the nightingale's ecstatic song) invites the human listener to pour forth his soul (breathe his last breath).

# Passion and Permanence in Keats's
## *Ode on a Grecian Urn*

### *by Charles I. Patterson*

Despite much that serves as corrective in three subsequent explicatory essays,[1] Professor H. W. Garrod's interpretation of Keats's *Ode on a Grecian Urn,* similar to an earlier interpretation by Robert Bridges, has continued to enjoy wide currency.[2] Professor Garrod, I think, offers an impoverished, fragmentary, and static reading of the poem. He states:

> The theme of what has gone before [before the last stanza] is the arrest of beauty, the fixity given by art to forms which in life are fluid and impermanent, and the appeal of art from the senses to the spirit. The theme of the final stanza is the relation of beauty to truth, to thought. Nothing has prepared the transition to this. . . . The figures of the Urn become for him, suddenly, a 'Cold Pastoral'—cold with the character of everything that is enduring. . . . The second half of the stanza—of which the first, marring seriously, as I think, the effect of all that has preceded, has called in question the appeal of art. . . . Down to the end of the fourth stanza there is a very perfect development of the governing idea—'the supremacy of ideal art over nature, because of its unchanging expression of perfection!' Perhaps the fourth stanza is more beautiful than any of the others—and more true. The trouble is

---

*"Passion and Permanence in Keats's* Ode on a Grecian Urn" *by Charles I. Patterson. From* ELH, XXI *(1954), 208–20. Revised by the author. Reprinted by permission of the author and The Johns Hopkins Press.*

[1] In Kenneth Burke, *A Grammar of Motives* (New York, 1935); Cleanth Brooks, *The Well Wrought Urn* (New York, 1947); C. M. Bowra, *The Romantic Imagination* (London, 1950).

[2] I had completed the present essay when Professor Earl R. Wasserman's *The Finer Tone: Keats' Major Poems* (Baltimore, 1953) came off the press. The second chapter therein gives the most detailed explication of the *Ode on a Grecian Urn* yet to appear. Although he and I agree in some particulars, there are very significant points of disagreement between our two interpretations. Space and my present aims preclude the presentation here of arguments to support my views against his extended exegesis, but I shall indicate a few points of difference. Both readings embrace the whole poem—beginning, middle, and end—and both consider the end an integral part of the poem, not a blemish upon it, as some critics have maintained.

that it is a little too true. Truth to his main theme has taken Keats
rather farther than he meant to go. . . . This pure cold art makes, in
fact, a less appeal to Keats than the Ode as a whole would pretend; and
when, in the lines that follow these lines, he indulges the jarring apostrophe 'Cold Pastoral' (for jarring it is,—we detect, do what we may,
some accidental undertone of depreciation), he has said more than he
meant—or wished to mean.[3]

It is impossible to accept this notion that the poem celebrates the
"supremacy" of art over nature, for its total poetic fabric supports a
much more comprehensive and virile interpretation. At the risk of
being labeled a Freudian, I earnestly contend that there is as much
eulogy of passion as of permanence in the Ode. Failure to recognize
both in their proper relationship results in this type of "broken-back"
reading—an interpretation which cannot embrace the whole and
which must therefore condemn a part of the poem to save itself. Such
a reading reduces the poem to a simple lyric of escape and makes of
the poet a young man unwilling to face life as it is. That Keats was no
such "pet lamb in a sentimental farce" there is ample evidence elsewhere in his poetry and in his letters.

The interpretation which I wish to suggest here, chiefly in opposition to one-sided readings like Mr. Garrod's, can be set forth briefly
without the aid of elaborate criteria. We need accept only a few basic
principles: a worthy lyric should achieve imaginative fusion of all its
materials, however diverse; it should be made up of fresh imagery and
diction; and it should indicate some solution to the human problems
it raises if solutions are possible. There are more complex exegetical
techniques, but this particular poem will give forth its richness if, as
method, we first strike a balance between the passion and the permanence, noting carefully the importance and the role of both in each
stanza, and then reduce the last statement equating truth and beauty
to its proper place in the whole.

In the first line of the poem Keats pointedly enunciates the duality
of his theme in a metaphor whose dual functions are neatly balanced.
By addressing the urn as a "still unravished bride of quietness," he
suggests its changeless ungenerative descent through the ages; it does
not reproduce itself, but remains itself and transmits itself and its
meaning directly. At the same time the metaphor strongly suggests a
real bride and the idea of marital consummation. She cannot remain
herself through the ages; she reproduces herself to transmit herself and
to fulfill her destiny. It is erroneous to assume that here Keats is
merely disparaging the bride of flesh wed to man and glorifying the
bride of marble wed to quietness. He could have achieved that simple

[3] *Keats* (Oxford, 1926), pp. 105–7. Allen Tate is another critic who considers the
last stanza out of harmony with the whole. T. S. Eliot has objections to it also.

effect more deftly with some other image than the richly ambivalent
*unravished bride,* which conveys, along with the inviolate, undisturbed
sanctity of the urn-bride, a hint of disparagement: It is natural for
brides to be possessed physically, to be "ravished," so to speak; it is un-
natural for them not to be. And this suggestion is strengthened by the
next line, where the urn is designated a "foster child of silence and
slow time." In the normal order of things the antithesis of *foster child*
is *natural child,* which the urn clearly is not; it was not generated by
silence and slow time, but adopted and nurtured by them. Only those
who cannot procreate their own offspring adopt others, and they do
so as a *second best.* Here in the very beginning of the poem is a clue
to Keats's real attitude toward the permanence of the urn and the
"supremacy" of art.

Having set in motion this tension between something unchanging
because it is dead and something transient because it is alive, and
having refrained from declaring preference, Keats designates the urn
a "sylvan historian," more potent than poetry to tell a tale in a wood-
land-picture-history. He then hastens into the turbulent passion that
dominates lines 5 to the end of the stanza, rhapsodizing upon the puls-
ing *life* depicted there, not upon the "historian" itself. The urn's
poignant appeal stems as much from the life it suggests as from its
permanence:

> What leaf-fring'd legend haunts about thy shape
>   Of deities or mortals, or of both,
>     In Tempe or the dales of Arcady?
> What men or gods are these? What maidens loth?
>   What mad pursuit? What struggle to escape?
>     What pipes and timbrels? What wild ecstasy?

The word *shape* in this context is highly significant. Is it only a "legend," a story in pictures, that haunts about its form? The term draws
attention to the outlines of the urn; and its shape, encompassing and
framing the mad pursuit and wild ecstasies of the men and maidens,
bears a haunting resemblance to the lines of the feminine body,[4] a re-

---

[4] Although Keats had no particular single urn in mind, we do know that he had
seen and admired several which can be identified. An examination of drawings and
photographs of them will lend credence to the possibility that their shape suggests
the outlines of the feminine body (see plates in Sir Sidney Colvin, *John Keats,* New
York, 1917). But there is resemblance not only in shape: the urn is a receptacle,
just as is the body of woman—the receptacle from which life springs (in a procession not unlike that on the urn). The connection in thought between the urn and
woman in her generative capacity is established by Keats in his first line. In nature
it is budding or ripening life that usually assumes the swelling shapeliness of the
urn, and we instinctively think of vitality and growth in connection with the curved
line (see note 7 below). There must be a reason for Keats's bringing together the

semblance already intimated, or at least prepared for, in the initial designation of the urn: *unravished bride.* The form of the urn is subtly appropriate to embrace and frame the virile picture of life presented on its surface, for human life unfolds and continues through the body of woman. When one sums up *unravished bride, child, haunts about thy shape, men, maidens loth, mad pursuit, struggle to escape,* and *wild ecstasy,* he amasses a formidable array of the imagery of physical passion—all presented with relish and sympathy. It balances and, in fact, overbalances the eulogy of permanence in *bride of quietness, foster child of silence, slow time, historian,* and *legend.* Keats's imagination seems to grasp and hold the urn in a plasm of feeling;[5] it seems to respire with slumbering energy. Though working with words, he presents this object as Rembrandt would in a picture, and projects it before us invested with silent, unmoving vitality.

This equipoise is continued in the second stanza. Although the "ditties of no tone" are superior to the "heard melodies," the former are imaginatively realized and therefore presuppose a living mind if they exist at all. As for the lover beneath the deathless-because-lifeless trees, who cannot kiss the maid who cannot fade, it is impossible to believe that Keats really envied him his dubious happiness or desired to exchange places with him. The word *cannot* (and variants), repeated seven times within eight lines (15–23), pointedly suggests impotence; and the leaves that cannot be shed suggest the fruit that cannot be born. This lad is in a good condition for a lover engraved on an urn; he is in a miserable plight for a flesh-and-blood lover of a flesh-and-blood maiden. The words *do not grieve* readily suggest that there is cause for grief, as do *though thou hast not thy bliss;* and the concluding statement is much less than full acquiescence in the situation, in fact, is partly an ironic offer of spurious comfort:

> For ever wilt thou love and she be fair!

Thus Keats continues to toy with his dual matter, but he neither asserts nor implies that lasting permanence is superior to transient passion.

Nor does he do so in the third stanza. In sum it expresses the wish that the passion, the piping, and the panting could be more enduring in actuality, not merely in representation. The emphasis

---

outlines of the urn as *framework* and the carvings as *center piece,* for he actually saw prototypes of his urn-figures among the Elgin Marbles, and could as readily have written an ode on a Grecian frieze or pediment except for a conscious or subconscious desire to represent them as encompassed by form suggesting vitality.

[5] Cf. "Cognition itself can only be understood to approach the real when conceived as operating within the sustaining medium of feeling," Elijah Jordan, *The Aesthetic Object* (Bloomington, 1937), p. 72.

is still upon the warmth, the turbulence, the life, especially at the end, where he impetuously calls for more human passion; he wishes it to *breathe*, be it noted, even though far above the transient earthly sphere. This is quite different from his preferring either to *be* the lover on the urn or to contemplate him rather than to be a lover in the world and to consummate love in the flesh. The stanza distinctly does not say that Keats, with his powerfully active senses and his then burning passion, prefers his love vicariously realized for permanence rather than actually experienced for vitality. Anyone who doubts this should re-read the love letters and the poems to Fanny Brawne.

The fourth stanza presents the imagistic and structural climax of the poem;[6] here is carried to its ultimate development the ability of art to stir the imagination to "see into the life of things." And this development leads the poet to an inevitable turning back from the ideal world to the actual. First, there is the sacrificial procession, with its fresh, vital picture of community life and religious ritual; it casts about the lovers their proper and meaningful background. Secondly, the poet is as fully identified with the world of the carvings as he ever allows himself to be, as is evidenced by his use of the word *these*, not *those*, in the first line, as if the figures in the procession are all about him. But the apex of imagistic power and at the same time the inescapable turning point are reached when the poet's imagination, completing the scene, creates for itself the deserted little town not pictured but from which the people in the procession must have come forth:

> Who are these coming to the sacrifice?
>    To what green altar, O mysterious priest,
> Lead'st thou that heifer lowing at the skies,
>    And all her silken flanks with garlands drest?
> What little town by river or sea shore,
>    Or mountain-built with peaceful citadel,
>       Is emptied of this folk, this pious morn?
> And, little town, thy streets for evermore
>    Will silent be; and not a soul to tell
>       Why thou art desolate, can e'er return.

This little town possesses, at one and the same time, the charm of the remote and the pitiableness of the desolate. It is like the fairy lands forlorn of the *Ode to a Nightingale*—utterly *lost* (as the root meaning of *forlorn* denotes), that is, beyond human reach; it is lost

---

[6] Professor Wasserman believes and cogently argues that the third stanza is both the climax (the point of Keats's identification of himself with the urn-world and all it signifies) and also the point of disintegration of this line of development, hence the point at which the poem takes a new direction (*op. cit.*, pp. 36–41).

at the end of a corridor of rare dreams which we can enter but briefly and where we remain not long. The hint of disparagement in the earlier silence, the foster parent of the urn, has now become unmistakable, though reluctant, derogation; for here *thy streets forevermore will silent be* is equated with *thou art desolate.* We have been carried into a world that is permanent, but permanently empty, just as the art on the urn is permanent but permanently lifeless. From our momentary viewpoint here, the world of the living, transient though it be, beckons in its realness and vitality. Keats has tried not to deceive us all along, has constantly reminded us that he is talking about carved figures, even when making them glow and come to life. Now he is about to make sure that we are put straight.

In the final stanza, therefore, he deliberately shatters the spell he has cast over us and ends his dual game. Henceforth he emphatically addresses this thing of beauty as just what it is, a Grecian urn:

> O Attic shape! Fair attitude! with brede
>> Of marble men and maidens overwrought,
> With forest branches and the trodden weed;
>> Thou, silent form, dost tease us out of thought
> As doth eternity: Cold Pastoral!
>> When old age shall this generation waste,
>> Thou shalt remain, in midst of other woe
> Than ours, a friend to man, to whom thou say'st,
>> Beauty is truth, truth beauty,—that is all
>> Ye know on earth, and all ye need to know.

This work of art has teased us "out of thought," that is, out of the world of the actual and into an ideal world in which we can momentarily identify ourselves imaginatively with life that is free of the particular imperfections of our lot here. But this ideal world is not free of *all* imperfection; it has very grave deficiencies, for it is lifeless, motionless, cold, unreal. At the very apex of our enjoyment of its permanence, we realize that it has these imperfections and that it exists only in conception. Hence we leave its desolate streets, which we could see but could not enter, indeed which no one will ever enter, and willingly return to the world of the actual. In the first lines of this stanza, attention is again centered upon the urn's physical outline, and the sexual suggestion returns with compelling insistence. The urn is designated an "Attic shape," a "fair attitude," with a "brede of marble men and maidens," a "silent form"; and it is in the midst of "this generation" (whose double meaning is played against "Cold Pastoral," as is that of *brede*). The cumulative effect of all these terms is to summon forth very, very delicately in the background the lines of the feminine form in all its vital richness—woman the eternal, holding deep within her the sum of all, the ability to recreate and transmit life.[7] As this image pervades the consciousness, the glowing carved figures, which have been vivified by the poet's imagination, recede and fade; they reassume their immobile, lifeless status on the urn. The words *Cold Pastoral* fall upon the apprehension like the tolling of a bell, placing the cold art at the opposite pole from the warm life. The brief journey into fairy land is over, and Keats unmistakably means for it to be over.

It is impossible to accept Professor Garrod's belief that the magnificent, controlled stroke of "Cold Pastoral" is an inadvertent disparagement of the previously glorified art, unintended by Keats. The inability of Professor Garrod's reading to embrace the last splendid stanza is the failure of the interpretation—not the failure of Keats at the height of his lyrical powers. For him contemplation of art, nay, even imaginative cognizance of it to the fullest, cannot supplant experience. Art is an adjunct to life, an aid, not a substitute. Art can enrich, illumine, and intensify actual contact with life, but never take its place. Hence the most important words in the stanza follow this emphatic shattering of the dream. The urn is now termed *a friend to man.* In that relation to the living, it shall remain in midst of "other woe" transmitting its message and meaning to other men born of woman, and born, it should be stressed, as a result of "generation." Here the far-reaching significance of the potent, ambivalent image in the first line of the poem can be seen to the fullest: Both the brides—the ravished and the unravished—play out their roles to the end. What the urn says it says *to men;* without them it could neither *be* nor *be heard,* for men made it in the first place, and more men must be born if it is to have an audience in the future. One of the glories of the poem is its so deftly handling the problem of the relation of art to life. I disagree entirely with Professor Bowra's belief (*op. cit.,* p. 148) that the poem presents only a "theory of art, a doctrine intended to explain his own creative experience" and not applicable beyond those confines. Of course, the poem does not present a complete philosophy; but Keats saw fit to conclude by stressing that the urn is *a friend to man,* not merely to the artist, and that it says something of vast importance to men.

What it says in this capacity can be explained briefly, and it may

[7] Cf. Coleridge, "The beautiful in [an] object may be referred to two elements . . . the first belonging to the shapely. . . . The curve line is a modification of the force from without by the force from within, or the spontaneous. These are not arbitrary symbols, but the language of nature, universal and intuitive" ("Fragment of an Essay on Beauty," appended to *Biographia Literaria,* ed. Shawcross, Oxford, 1907, II, 251). "[Beauty] is, in the abstract, the unity of the manifold, the coalescence of the diverse; in the concrete, it is the union of the shapely (*formosum*) with the vital" ("On Poesy or Art," appended to *B. L.,* II, 257).

be neither new nor profound; but it will make sense in the light of human experience. That is always the point of view from which Keats works and the pole star that charts his course, even in and out of the fairy lands he frequents. Keats proclaimed several times that the poet speaks to men, not to himself or to other artists. Even in the early *Sleep and Poetry* (1816) Keats has said that the great purpose of poetry was "To soothe the cares, and lift the thoughts of man." And in lines added to *The Fall of Hyperion* Keats states:

> Sure a poet is a sage;
> A humanist, physician to all men.          (189–90)

A few lines later, the priestess Moneta comments:

> The poet and the dreamer are distinct,
> Diverse, sheer opposite, antipodes.          (199–200)

No sage, no physician to the human spirit, prescribes that men attempt to dream themselves into happiness by contemplating the "superiority" of works of art over experience rather than by participating in experience. Keats repeats again and again in his letters: "Nothing ever becomes real till it is experienced" (letter to George and Georgiana Keats, February 14–18, 1819). This, of course, means *experienced and understood*. He had written shortly before: "I never can feel certain of any truth but from a clear perception of its beauty" (letter to George and Georgiana Keats, December, 1818). To Keats this clear perception of beauty came with imaginative insight into the essential nature of an entity, and this deep awareness of the real truth of things is the only way to happiness, as is clear from his statement in *Endymion* that happiness is "fellowship with essence" (I, 779). Now for Keats, especially the Keats of 1819, *essence* is more like Aristotle's *Idea*[8] than like Plato's; that is, Keats's *essence*, like Aristotle's *Idea*, exists either in close relationship with an object or in a mind, while Plato's *Idea* is an absolute in itself, apart from mind or object. Actually, Keats's *essence* has a kinship with Hegel's conception of the *real*, for the poet's ultimate reality most often seems to be the life force unfolding itself in and through phenomena. Keats does not reveal a sufficiently serious and abiding affinity with

[8] Without invoking the name of Aristotle but mentioning Keats's "unconcern for Plato," Professor Jacob D. Wigod (*PMLA*, LXVIII, September, 1953, 779–90) interprets *essence* very nearly as I do and indicates a reading of *Endymion* in harmony with that meaning of the word. He opposes the extent to which Platonic and Neo-Platonic interpretations of *Endymion* were carried by Colvin, Bridges, De Selincourt, Murry, and Thorpe. Professor Walter Jackson Bate has expressed a view of Keats's poetry as a whole which agrees largely with Professor Wigod's view (*Criticism: The Major Texts*, New York, 1952, pp. 347–48).

Neo-Platonism[9] to do what Professor Bowra (*op. cit.,* p. 141) con-
tends—use the urn as a means of sustaining himself more than momentarily in an unchanging, timeless sphere (although he may toy
with the notion of remaining there). Keats's poetry feeds on his
sensory realization of time and phenomena, expresses itself in concrete images of time and phenomena; it eschews abstractions very
pointedly. It is as difficult to believe that for Keats in 1819 the real
is an abstract, absolute, unchanging world, typified by the carved
figures on the urn, as it is difficult to make such an interpretation
embrace the magnificent concluding stanza, where he puts art in its
place (and no inglorious place it is).

What we must do, I think, to clarify what the urn says to Keats
and to all men is to find some common element among *essence,
beauty, truth,* and *experience* as Keats uses these terms. If we recall
the duality of his theme in the poem, we can be sure that he treats of
two kinds of experience: (1) human love in actuality, and (2) the
appreciation of an imaginary representation of several human activi-
ties—love, art (in the music of the pipes), community life, and religious ritual—which together represent nearly all the human funda-
mentals. The representation is projected on an urn resembling the
outlines of the feminine figure. The two kinds of experience are thus
related. By contemplating this picture *in this framework* men can see,
as Keats came to see, the essence of both love and art. The essence of
art is mimesis; in the appreciation of it we must not confuse it with
the actual, for then we cannot grasp its meaning and significance.
Just as he is about to comment on the meaning of the art-experience
in the poem, Keats reminds us that the art involved is merely a carved
scene of marble men and maidens—a cold pastoral. He knows that
it alone can never satisfy us completely, and he is here rejecting it
*as reality;* it is only an imitation of reality, "a shadow of a magnitude,"
as he says in the sonnet on the Elgin Marbles. But this work of art
can tell us something important about the real experience in the
realm of the actual, the love passion that is so fleeting and transient,
can mitigate our pain that it is so. That is, the essence of physical
love is participation in the life force and the continuing life process;
only the individual instance is transient and short-lived, not physical
love in all human life of all time. The fiery heat of desire, that "leaves
a heart high-sorrowful and cloy'd," is only its immediate form of
being, not its essential reality. In essence it is the life force that
pervades and interfuses phenomena, and it is enduring and real, and
therefore "true," for Keats says that the urn shall remain in midst

[9] Professor Wasserman has stated, "Keats did not believe the world itself to be
symbolic; it is not an imperfect shadow of the real, where all values reside . . ."
(*op. cit.,* p. 53).

of other life than ours, not in midst of nothing. "Beauty is truth," then, means that beauty is total reality properly understood; that is, beauty is the true significance of things in our world and in the ideal one, and we perceive this beauty when we neither mistake art for life nor mistake the ever-changing phenomena of life for the great, enduring organic reality in which they inhere. Keats is saying that beauty lies in the real world of men,[10] not merely in art and in the fairy lands of fancy. *To Autumn,* written a few months later, is an emphatic statement of his belief in the living beauty of the phenomenal world. But the art-experience of the urn, understood for just what it is worth and no more, has helped his cognitive imagination to realize this truth. The urn has been to his mind what light is to the eye, has made insight possible.[11] Hence, the poem ends in a tone of noble resignation, as if his mind had pierced to the heart of our life here on earth, and had accepted *it*—not the spurious comfort of an imaginary escape from its imperfections.

The meaningfulness and range of the poem, along with its controlled execution and powerfully suggestive imagery, entitle it to a high place among Keats's great odes. It lacks the even finish and extreme perfection of *To Autumn* but is much superior in these qualities to the *Ode to a Nightingale* despite the magic passages in the latter and the similarities of over-all structure. In fact, the *Ode on a Grecian Urn* may deserve to rank first in the group if viewed in something approaching its true complexity and human wisdom.

[10] Here Professor Wasserman and I are in direct opposition, for he holds that the poem does not mean to assert that beauty is truth in the phenomenal world (*op. cit.,* pp. 60–62).

[11] Cf. Coleridge's dictum: "As light to the eye, even such is beauty to the mind. . . . Hence the Greeks called a beautiful object . . . [a] *calling on* the soul" ("Principles of Genial Criticism," appended to *B.L.,* II, 243).

# Keats's Ideal in the *Ode on a Grecian Urn*

## *by Jacob Wigod*

Rooted in awareness of pain and flux, Keats's odes of 1819 reveal the poet's desire to escape the painful actual and seek repose in beauty, in the ideal. More than any other of the odes, the implicit subject of the *Ode on a Grecian Urn* is the ideal itself. While the permanence of art is the poet's bulwark against flux, it is not the ultimate perfection that he seeks. Too many inner tensions, as the poem develops, shape the ideal into something much more complex, unattainable in either life or art since it encompasses *both* life and art. Keats's attempt to define this ideal accounts for the difficulty of the concluding lines. The purpose of this paper is to try to illuminate Keats's mode of thought and feeling as he wrote the poem and thereby, perhaps, to approach more closely his meaning.[1]

In the first stanza Keats or the speaker, standing apart as it were, gazes at the urn contemplatively. It is an object to muse upon, isolated in the dignity of its ancientness—whole, undisturbed, quiet. The observer is aware that at *his* point in time it exists for him but that it has existed for countless generations before him. More than that, it is a "sylvan historian" that speaks to him silently out of the past, relating a "leaf-fringed legend" of long ago, when gods walked in the vales of Tempe and Arcadia. Though the urn itself is silent, the poet sees that its detail depicts a revelry—mad pursuit, struggle to escape, pipes and

---

"Keats's Ideal in the Ode on a Grecian Urn" by Jacob Wigod. Reprinted by permission of the Modern Language Association from PMLA, LXXII (1957), 113–21.

[1] Among recent critics Kenneth Burke, Cleanth Brooks, Middleton Murry, Allen Tate, and Earl Wasserman all read the ode as a form of dramatic or symbolic action. There are, however, at least two distinct approaches. Burke, Brooks, and Tate are concerned with the structure of the poem itself; on the other hand, Murry and Wasserman, while concentrating on the poem, also try to infer from earlier writings the *poet's* framework of thought and emotion. The second method has its pitfalls but when reasonably pursued is, I believe, the best way to study the work of a Romantic poet. Keats is as much a part of the ode as the urn itself. Some of the tension and urgency of the poem is lost when it is examined simply as artifact. Burke misreads the poem, while Brooks and Tate—though (or because) they are conservative—miss the underlying tension. The present paper is necessary because there are disturbing flaws in the readings of both Murry and Wasserman.

timbrels, wild ecstasy. He asks the questions that any curious observer
might ask: What do these actions signify? Who are these men or gods?
Who are these maidens?

As he asks these questions, he comes closer and imaginatively enters
into the scene before his eyes. In the second stanza, therefore, the urn
as object fades from sight; the poet gives us, instead, a close-up of its
detail. He accepts now the anonymity of these figures, men or gods;
indeed takes pleasure in their anonymity and silence, since the keen
delight of imagining is left to him:

> Heard melodies are sweet, but those unheard
> Are sweeter; therefore, ye soft pipes, play on;
> Not to the sensual ear, but, more endear'd,
> Pipe to the spirit ditties of no tone.

Since they are unknown, the figures assume a general identity that
verges on the symbolic. The fair youth piping songs beneath the trees,
since he is of unknown place and unknown time, may be regarded as
the artist—poet or musician—of any place and any time. So the lover
pursuing the maiden may be regarded as any lover and the maiden
as any beautiful woman who is loved; or, more broadly, these figures
are symbolic of love and beauty. In the real world, the poet has
mourned, Beauty cannot keep her lustrous eyes (*Ode to a Nightingale*)
and the lover's mistress dwells with Beauty that must die (*Ode on
Melancholy*). But the tree, piper, lover, and maiden will always be
enjoying or about to enjoy: the tree, its green leaves; the piper, his
song; the lover, his pursuit and passion and the hope of winning his
bliss; the maiden, her spirited youth and radiant beauty. The grace-
ful movement and living action of human creatures—moments of
being and becoming, aspiration and growth—have been caught and
held, suspended permanently in art.

In the third stanza the poet rejoices in the ripeness that has been
rescued from time. Yet his rejoicing is not unmixed with nostalgia and
sorrow, reflected in the repetition of "happy," a word that bears much
emotional stress in the odes. He longs for the ideal in nature, art, and
love as they are represented on the urn (ll. 21–27). The lines about
love are almost unbearable in the intensity of their yearning. His grief
comes to the surface and with it the painful recognition of the vast
unbridgeable gulf separating the ideal from the real—the perpetual
renewal of warm, young love on the urn from the throes and fever of
breathing human passion in real life.

This sorrow pervades the following stanza and unites it emotionally
with what has preceded, though it is unrelated thematically. We are,
I suppose, to imagine the poet turning to another scene depicted on
the urn, for he is once more the curious observer asking particular

questions. This scene as the poet presents it to us—the priest leading
the heifer to sacrifice—is most lifelike in its detail:

> Who are these coming to the sacrifice?
> To what green altar, O mysterious priest,
> Lead'st thou that heifer lowing at the skies,
>     And all her silken flanks with garlands drest?

Keats felt, no doubt, that the poem had to be rounded off by a
stanza that would give the reader a more complete sense of time and
place, a more fixed impression of that far-off Grecian age in which the
urn itself was fashioned. So, though the stanza is not about the permanence of nature, youth, love, and beauty in art and its transiency
in the real world, the description of the pagan ritual creates in our
minds a definite picture of the society in which these human figures
moved. The little town "by river or sea shore, / Or mountain-built
with peaceful citadel" further widens our knowledge of background.
And the poet's feeling for the little town further deepens the compassion that runs through the whole poem:

> And, little town, thy streets for evermore
> Will silent be; and not a soul to tell
> Why thou art desolate can e'er return.

These lines are somehow more moving, even, than the poet's compassion for melodist, lover, and maiden. The town in all its desolation suggests total silence, just as the sacrificial rite, the priest leading
the heifer lowing at the skies, suggests ancientness and slow time.

In the last stanza the poet again stands apart from the object. He
is no longer absorbed in it; it stands before him, a "shape," an "attitude," a "silent form." Its timelessness is awe-inspiring: it teases him
out of thought as does eternity.[2] Standing silent and inscrutable, it is

---

[2] There are, it seems to me, at least two other possible meanings for this difficult
line (44): first, that the poet's total absorption in the urn precluded thought, so
powerful was his aesthetic experience; second, that the urn was a means of escape
from thought about the pain, the conflict of good and evil in human existence. Of
these two interpretations I am inclined to think the first more likely.

This expression ("tease us out of thought") also occurs in the *Epistle to John
Hamilton Reynolds* (ll. 76–77). The context is:

> Oh never will the prize,
> High reason, and the lore of good and ill
> Be my award. Things cannot to the will
> Be settled, but they tease us out of thought.

I confess I do not know exactly what Keats means here. I should guess that "high
reason and the lore of good and ill" are the "things" that "cannot to the will be
settled." That is, he cannot determine to acquire high reason and the lore of good
and ill without finding that these aspirations are too immense, too much for his
intellect to grasp (like the urn, like eternity) at once; hence, he is teased out of
thought.

too large an object for human comprehension in the sense that, while it records history ("sylvan historian"), it possesses a long history of its own; it spans innumerable generations, innumerable creations and destroyings. We cannot *think* about it, we can only *wonder* at it as we wonder at eternity. It shares the coldness of eternity—Cold Pastoral! —unfeeling, imperturbable, the figures etched on its surface frozen, requiring a meeting of the mind, an active imagination, to give them warm life. The poet's mood at this point is comparable to his feeling in the *Ode to a Nightingale,* after the spell of the nightingale's song is broken: "Forlorn! the very word is like a bell / To toll me back from thee to my sole self!" In the midst of ecstasy (imaginative flight) he experiences joy and exultation, but he always faces reality at the end. "A sense of real things comes doubly strong . . . like a muddy stream" (*Sleep and Poetry*); he makes the long "journey homeward to habitual self" (*Endymion*); fancy is a "deceiving elf" (*Ode to a Nightingale*); and the urn is a cold pastoral. Yet even when absorbed in the urn, he knew that art was not so fine as life, just as marble men and maidens are not so fine as breathing human beings.

The principal tension in the poem comes from this awareness that what he most enjoys in life—warm, youthful sensuousness, love and beauty—must be spontaneous and fluid, ever-changing, if they are to retain their special vitality and charm. They belong to life, not to art. Art may resist flux and perpetuate lover and maiden, but, dead and cold in itself, it can only *represent* life. No matter how great an effort of the imagination is made to endow these figures with breathing, sensuous life, they remain but a semblance of life, a "brede of marble men and maidens." So he feels compassion not only for the lover who will grow old and the beautiful woman that will lose her lustrous eyes in real life (*Ode to a Nightingale*), but also, in art, for the lover who will never attain his goal and for the town that will be forever desolate.

He wanted, then, two irreconcilable things: life in its ever-changing fullness—the lover's ardor, the flush on the maiden's cheek, her sparkling eyes, her alternating moods and caprices—and he wanted to arrest these ripe moments and hold them permanently. The second desire clearly stems from the first. It is the result of his sheer zest for living, the natural gusto with which he seized life, and the accompanying profoundly melancholy awareness that all passes, all is flux. Art was to embody his ideal but, ironically, he found it deficient in life. Nervous unrest in life was replaced by placidity and calm in art; passion and fever, by tranquillity; disorder and chaos, by order and harmony; flux, by permanence. Since life is a flow and subsists in change, the flow of blood within and the flow of time and circumstance without, in addition to the constant physical action of the body, then the essential nature and vitality of life itself is negated when transfixed in art. There is a stoppage of the circulation, or stasis, and a suspension of both time and circumstance. Nothing is left but form.

In life the passage of time brings completion. Unless a change in relationship occurs or untoward circumstance intervenes, the lover in real life consummates his love and thereby wins his bliss; while the sculptured lover, subject neither to chance nor change, is always about to enjoy, but never enjoys. Keats would certainly choose to be the lover pillowed on his fair love's ripening breast despite the "sweet unrest." He would first desire the breathing reality even though he (and she) could not have the steadfastness of a star or even certainty of the immediate future. But in the very midst of joy he is conscious that in time's continuum beauty fades, man and woman grow old. Time has its revenges, brings in its train the final completion, death. What he really desires is the ripeness of youth, its joy and bliss, lasting forever. His ideal, in short, is the best of both worlds, what he can have neither in life nor in art alone.[3]

Cold pastoral! One can almost feel the arrow-sharp disappointment as the magic is dispelled and the warmth of the poet's absorption in the urn is replaced by the chill of his objective scrutiny. A familiar pattern in Keats—initial detachment leading to absorption in the dream and the ideal, followed by rejection—has been repeated.[4] The two words seem final and irrevocable, destructive of all that has gone before. They are, however, an honest expression of *part* of the poet's whole aesthetic experience. Balance is restored by the concluding affirmation, which signifies that the poet has made the necessary compromise. He realizes that the urn is indeed a cold pastoral, several removes from life, but that it is nonetheless beautiful.

To Keats beauty, the object of his pursuit in *Endymion* and his solace in *Hyperion*, was an attribute of the ideal. By sympathizing with humanity and by directly experiencing the real, Endymion had won Cynthia, or ideal beauty, for his bride. *Endymion* was allegorical

---

[3] Wasserman sees the poet's conception in a similar light: "No one," he writes, "will deny that the ode, like most of Keats' poems, deals with the human and mutable on the one hand, and the immortal and essential on the other; and that what it states has something to do with both an opposition and a fusion of these two states." This delicate balancing at the very bourne of heaven, this "paradoxical essence" is, in Wasserman's view, "the central principle of Keats' visions." He calls it—borrowing a term from Kenneth Burke—"mystic oxymoron." Accordingly, "although the ode is a symbolic action in terms of an urn, its intrinsic theme is that region where earth and the ethereal, light and darkness, time and no-time become one; and what the symbolic drama ultimately discovers is the way in which art (the urn) relates man to that region" (*The Finer Tone*, The Johns Hopkins Press, 1953, pp. 14–16).

[4] Cf. *Sleep and Poetry*, ll. 47–162; *Endymion*, II, 273–80; the original conclusion of *The Eve of St. Agnes*; and *Ode to a Nightingale*.

of the artist's quest for the ideal, embodied in Cynthia the moon-god-dess. In the *Ode on a Grecian Urn* beauty, though intrinsically de-sirable, is not a passive ideal to be reached for in a rarer atmosphere than the earth's; rather, like the nightingale's song, it possesses active power to soothe everyman's mortal pain.[5] Hence the poet addresses the urn:

> When old age shall this generation waste,
> Thou shalt remain, in midst of other woe
> Than ours, a friend to man, to whom thou say'st,
> Beauty is truth, truth beauty,—that is all
> Ye know on earth, and all ye need to know.[6]

Beauty is truth, truth beauty: the generalization is so dazzling that it almost blinds us. We cannot, of course, determine precisely what the poet means, but we can try first to find his meaning in the context of

[5] The climax occurs at this point of tragic awareness, in the final stanza. Wasser-man is surely wrong in assuming that the climax occurs at the end of the third stanza. Illuminating Keats's conception of the ideal, he makes no allowance for his growth. He holds that ideas expressed in the letter to Bailey about the imagination (Nov. 22, 1817) together with important passages in *Endymion* (1817)—principally, the "pleasure thermometer" (I, 777 ff.) and the "Hymn to Pan"—constitute both the framework in which the ode is set and the key to its meaning. In the ode, the po-et's "ascent" from nature (the boughs) to music (the piper's song) to love (lover and maiden) parallels the ascent to the "chief intensity" in *Endymion* (I, 777 ff.). The poet, by the close of the third stanza, achieves a complete "empathic entrance into essence" ("fellowship with essence") and so reaches heaven's bourne. The statement "Beauty is truth, truth beauty," according to Wasserman, would logically occur at this point, if it were "the total intention of the poem," since that is what the poem up to that point has been saying. "The intention of the poem," he decides finally, "must be to hold up art as the source of the highest form of wisdom," since the urn speaks the "aphorism" in the last stanza (pp. 37–39, 49). Thus the conflict within the poet, which should be pinpointed since it is the drama of the poem, is allowed to fade into the background. In 1817, to be sure, Keats's subject was young love and the ideal beauty that he would win by humanitarian sympathy. His poetic ladder of ascent (*Endymion*, I, 777 ff.) was still a luxury, a "pleasure thermometer"—a plan rather than a deed accomplished—and his humanitarianism a Wordsworthian en-dowment. But by 1819 the axiom had been proved on his pulses: in the interim he had experienced suffering, and he had written the fragment of an epic. His subject now was the melancholy of change and pain, and the ideal (the nightingale's song, the urn) was not so much an object of pursuit as an active comforter of human suffering. The right key to the meaning of the ode is not *Endymion* but, as Murry saw, the letter on the Vale of Soul-Making (Feb. 14–May 3, 1819).

[6] That Keats meant the urn to speak the last two lines is clear from the tran-scripts made by Charles Brown and Richard Woodhouse (Houghton Library), and the transcripts of George Keats (British Museum) and Dilke (Hampstead House). Punctuation in all transcripts is basically as follows: "Beauty is Truth,—Truth Beauty,—that is all / Ye know on earth, and all ye need to know" (Brown). See Alvin Whitley, "The Message of the Grecian Urn," *Keats-Shelley Memorial Bulletin*, No. 5, ed. Dorothy Hewlett (London, 1953), pp. 1–3.

the poem itself. "Truth" is the more difficult word to explain. Clearly, it is not the same as the tragic truth of *Hyperion* and the *Epistle to John Hamilton Reynolds*; it has nothing to do with pain or the strife of good and evil. Since the ode is about a work of art that embodies the ideal, "truth" here may mean "highest value," or "highest reality" in the sense closest to "the ideal." Similarly, "beauty" in the ode is not synonymous with that beauty in *Hyperion* which mirrored the wisdom, wrought in agony, of Apollo and the inner grace and knowledge of the Olympians. Rather, the ode reveals a twofold conception of beauty: first, the warm, pulsating beauty of lover and maiden in real life, which Keats had portrayed so glowingly in *Isabella* and *The Eve of St. Agnes*; and second, the beauty of art, which can preserve and give some idea of the original living, sensuous human beings. What he seems to be saying, then, is that the vision of life itself in full blossom, ardent and unselfconscious, is to be cherished as the ultimate reality: it is all (that is, the utmost) man knows on earth and all he needs to know.[7]

Filling in gaps here and there, we can also, I think, deduce from the poem Keats's line of reasoning about the beauty of art. Through perception and, above all, expression of beauty the "poor forked creature," man, attains the peak of his cultural development. A work of art like the urn represents man's highest point above the animal since it is a manifestation of the spirit. (Therefore, the poet asks "What men *or gods* are these?" and desires the pipes to play on, "not to the sensual ear" but to "the spirit ditties of no tone.") Once in ancient Greece a sculptor captured and locked fast the youthful ecstasy of piper, lover, and maiden for all succeeding generations of men to see and wonder at and enjoy. Thus man can perpetuate himself and win the same immortality in art that the nightingale achieves by its song.

Although the line "Beauty is truth, truth beauty . . ." can bear all the weight of interpretation I have laid upon it, it is nonetheless a brilliant failure. Some readers have considered the affirmation a

---

[7] Kenneth Burke assumes that "beauty" is "the essential word of art or poetry" and that "truth" is the essential word of knowledge or science. Then he tries to reconcile the "oracle's" statement that "Poetry is science, science poetry" by showing how, in five stanzas, the transformation was made which enabled "the romantic philosophy of a romantic poet to transcend itself" (*A Grammar of Motives*, New York, 1945, pp. 447–62). He does so with extraordinary agility and insight, but his conclusion (p. 462) is unconvincing. One feels, with Tate, that "Mr. Burke's own dialectical skill leads him to consider the poem, when he is through with it, a philosophical discourse" (*On the Limits of Poetry*, New York, 1948, p. 178). Crude equations like this cannot contain an imaginative poet's *vision*. Keats's line elicits a wide range of response. I. A. Richards would object to any such "translation"; he would say that Burke himself has failed to distinguish between *emotive* and *scientific* statement (*Principles of Literary Criticism*, London, 1925, p. 267).

meaningless appendage; on the contrary, I believe the poet tries to say too much.[8] The word "truth" implies a final answer which the poem itself does not give; I feel that the poet is trying to say more in the concluding lines than he has said in the course of the whole poem. Too much has to be inferred. The structure and content of the poem will admit of no such all-embracing generalization.[9] Keats tries to condense in five words what Tolstoy later said successfully in *War and Peace,* about the beauty of life in full flow, all that man can know on earth. Tolstoy was detached and saw human existence, as someone has remarked, with the eyes of God. He remained above, looking down, while he allowed himself ample space and time. Keats, on the other hand, is much too close to the object; he cannot escape absorption in his vision of the ideal; and his emotional participation in the happiness of the figures portrayed on the urn forms a strange contrast to the final detached, impersonal declaration. And in these last, brief words he wants to say something about the beauty of art as well as the beauty of life's youth, love, and spring! It is the mark of his genius that he nearly succeeds.

What Keats is really stating, prematurely in the poem, is his "favorite speculation," which he had recorded for Bailey in November, 1817. Then he had said: "What the imagination seizes as Beauty must be truth. . . . The Imagination may be compared to Adam's dream—he awoke and found it truth. . . . It is a 'Vision in the form of Youth,' a Shadow of reality to come." This idea was joined to "another favorite speculation" of his, "that we shall enjoy ourselves hereafter by having what we called happiness on Earth repeated in a finer tone and so

---

[8] I believe, with Richards, that the line is "the expression of a certain blend of feelings" (*Practical Criticism,* London, 1929, p. 187).

[9] Cleanth Brooks, however, considers the lines to be a fitting conclusion. He would waive the "question of the scientific or philosophic truth of the lines" (which Burke tries to resolve), in favor of applying the principle of "dramatic propriety." The urn's speech, "modified by the total context of the poem," is as appropriate as the speech of a character in a drama. The urn, he concludes, says that " 'formed experience,' imaginative insight, embodies the basic and fundamental perception of man and nature. The urn is beautiful, and yet its beauty is based—what else is the poem concerned with?—on an imaginative perception of essentials. Such a vision is beautiful but it is also true" (*The Well Wrought Urn,* New York, 1947, pp. 140–42, 150–51). On the other hand, Murry and Tate agree with T. S. Eliot that "*in the context of the poem itself*" the lines appear to be a blemish, an intrusion; for Murry, they "disturb the subtle harmony of the poem" (*The Mystery of Keats,* London, 1949, pp. 163–64). Tate considers them a "radical violation" in the "set limits" of the ode: "The poem gets out of form," a "break in 'point of view' occurs" (pp. 179–80). Whereas Brooks is perhaps too detached to do justice to the stresses in the poem, Murry is too absorbed. In his worship of Keats he tends to view the poem almost as mystical utterance, in which "Beauty is truth, truth beauty" becomes a saying of the same order as "God is Love" (p. 174). Consequently, the question of meaning is dissolved in wonder and mystery.

repeated. . . . Adam's dream will do here and seems to be a conviction that Imagination and its empyreal reflection is the same as
human life and its Spiritual repetition." [10]

Now if we turn to the lines again, they may appear in their true
light, as an affirmation of faith:[11]

> Beauty is truth, truth beauty,—that is all
> Ye know on earth, and all ye need to know.

Since faith is outside the poem and has been superimposed, as it were,
these lines can be read only partially within the context of the poem.
The poet's vision, like Adam's dream, controls the ode at this point
and transcends, at the same time that it includes, all that has gone
before. We now understand why the poet declares that the urn will
always remain a friend to suffering man. What solace, we might have
asked, can an urn that depicts youth, love, and merriment, give to
aging and suffering humanity whose burdens increase as youth fades
into the past? An apparent contradiction is resolved when we consider
the transient beauty portrayed on the urn as "a Shadow of reality to
come." Old age will indeed rejoice and be comforted in the knowledge
that this "Vision in the form of Youth" will be a permanent reality
in the next world. Meanwhile actual beauty, fleeting as it is, is all
man knows *on earth,* and all he needs to know. But, speaks the poet's
faith, "we shall enjoy ourselves hereafter by having what we called
happiness on Earth repeated in a finer tone and so repeated."

Art has transcended natural laws of time and flux; out of time, the
artist has created the timeless; out of flux, the permanent. The urn
itself, like Keats's poetry, was "a Vision in the form of Youth," an
"empyreal reflection" of the imagination. More specifically, it was the
objective correlative of that faith in beauty which, throughout his
poetry, underlies Keats's conception of the ideal. He wanted desper-
ately to extend to life itself the permanence of this ideal which he
cherished in myth, art, and poetry. To do so required firm religious
convictions, an unwavering belief in man's immortality, but his natural skepticism militated against orthodoxy. In his last year he still
"longed to believe in immortality." While he fluctuated in his religious belief, he had to struggle sometimes even to maintain wholehearted faith in the ideal. Harsh actuality battered and burst through

[10] Cf. Newell Ford, *The Prefigurative Imagination of John Keats* (Stanford Univ.
Press, 1951), pp. 138–40. *Letters,* ed. M. Buxton Forman, 4th ed. (Oxford, 1952),
p. 67.

[11] I. A. Richards would call a statement like "Beauty is truth . . ." a "pseudo-
statement," by which he means in some instances something very close to "an
expression of faith." It is the poet's way of ordering and controlling his experience,
emotions, and attitudes (*Science and Poetry,* London, 1926, pp. 58–59).

his defenses: the urn becomes a "cold pastoral," the nightingale's song, a "plaintive anthem." He asks, at the end of the *Ode to a Nightingale*: "Was it a vision or a waking dream?" The word "vision" belongs to the language of faith and refers to the ideal. By affirmations of faith in the urn and the nightingale ("Thou wast not born for death, immortal Bird!"), he strove to believe against all doubts in the ideal, with the same fervor with which he prayed for the spiritual repetition of human life.

# Romance and Reality: Continuity and Growth in Keats's View of Art

## by *Albert Gérard*

. . . It is now time to turn to the *Ode on a Grecian Urn,* which Keats wrote after another year of experience and meditation. It is a commonplace of Keats criticism that the *Ode* exalts, as Bridges put it, "the supremacy of ideal art over Nature, because of its unchanging expression of perfection," [1] or, to borrow Murry's formula, "the supremacy of the changeless and, in the strict metaphysical sense, eternal world of the imagination." [2] This is a rather simple interpretation of a poem whose complexity few people are likely to deny; the view I want to submit is that the main theme of the *Ode* is not the supremacy of art over life, but rather the function of art in life.

The subject matter of the poem centers round the two carved scenes on which Keats chooses to comment.[3] The main theme of the first scene is love as idealized through art. As Wasserman has shown in his most elaborate analysis,[4] stanza II and the first seven lines of stanza III describe with growing intensity a state of perfect bliss (which may have mystical significance, although this is by no means obvious when we consider the poem in isolation), but it should be

"*Romance and Reality: Continuity and Growth in Keats's View of Art*" by Albert Gérard. From Keats-Shelley Journal, XI *(1962), 17–29. Reprinted by permission of the author and the editor of* Keats-Shelley Journal. *The first part of the essay, on the verse epistle to J. H. Reynolds, is here omitted. The complete essay has been reprinted in M. Gérard's* English Romantic Poetry *(Berkeley and Los Angeles: University of California Press, 1968).*

[1] Introduction to *Poems of John Keats,* ed. G. Thorn Drury (London, 1896), quoted by H. W. Garrod in *Keats,* 2nd ed. (Oxford, 1957), p. 103.

[2] J. M. Murry, *Keats* (London, 1955), p. 320.

[3] I cannot agree with Spitzer's view that stanza I and stanzas II and III deal with two different scenes. It seems to me obvious that the apostrophe "ye soft pipes, play on" refers back to the pipes of the first stanza, while the bold lover "winning near the goal" must be one of the competitors in the "mad pursuit." Cf. L. Spitzer, "The 'Ode on a Grecian Urn,' or Content vs. Metagrammar," *Comparative Literature,* VII (Summer 1955), 203–25.

[4] E. R. Wasserman, *The Finer Tone: Keats' Major Poems* (Baltimore, 1953).

added that this happiness is of a kind likely to gratify Keats's "exquisite sense of the luxurious" rather than his "love for philosophy." It prolongs the type of inspiration which gave birth to the *Ode to Psyche*. Keats's description of Eros and Psyche was focused on the particular moment when gratification has brought quietness, while desire and tenderness have not yet been destroyed by surfeit:

> They lay calm-breathing on the bedded grass;
>> Their arms embraced, and their pinions too;
>> Their lips touch'd not, but had not bade adieu,
> As if disjoined by soft-handed slumber,
> And ready still past kisses to outnumber
>> At tender eye-dawn of aurorean love.      (lines 15–20)

The artist of the Grecian Urn has likewise made immortal an intensity of passion which is essentially transient.

The climax in Keats's growing identification occurs in the first seven lines of the third stanza. But the path is not so smooth as a careless reading might suggest. In this respect, the ambivalence of the second part of stanza II should be noted:

> Fair youth, beneath the trees, thou canst not leave
>> Thy song, nor ever can those trees be bare;
>> Bold Lover, *never, never canst thou kiss*,
> Though winning near the goal—yet, do not grieve;
>> She cannot fade, *though thou hast not thy bliss*.

The italicized passages are negative in meaning, but even the positive statements are couched in negative terms. It sounds as if the poet were in two minds about the happiness that he is describing: while envying and projecting himself into the everlasting passion which animates the lover, he cannot help realizing that it is somehow incomplete since it will never reach fulfilment. The precarious poise expressed in those five lines soon gives way, however, to full-hearted acquiescence, as Keats drops all mention of the negative side of the lover's predicament and celebrates the happiness of everlasting desire.

The climactic picture in stanza III is one of pure harmony. The Urn, *qua* work of art, fixes for ever what is essentially transient, and the connected secondary motifs of nature and music only strengthen the impression of flawless perfection on which the description of the lover concludes. Whether, then, the artist who carved the urn intended his characters to represent "deities or mortals," "men or gods," hardly matters: their "for ever panting" love is "all . . . human passion far above"; if they were intended as men, art has idealized them and made them like gods in their eternal youth. Within the framework of the poem, the Romantic *Sehnsucht,* the dream of perfection, has once more come true. But it is typical of Keats's mature integrity that he makes no attempt to evade reality by seeking to prolong the dream and stay in that blessed spot, where in Chaucer's words, "grene and lusty May shal ever endure." [5] On the contrary, the sheer intensity of the scene recalls to his mind the heartbreak of actual life. And the grammar of the last six lines of stanza III, in which the two divergent trends of thought are fused into one single sentence, shows that the climactic realization of the dream is coinstantaneous with the anticlimactic awareness of life as it actually is. This sestet thus points with nearly unbearable pathos to the unbridged gap between the ideal and the actual, between art and life.

But is this gap unbridgeable? Is it due to the very nature of art? It might seem so, since the urn has created beauty only by suppressing the unavoidable condition of life: it has suppressed the dynamism which leads both to fulfilment and decay, as well as the tensions and the contradictions which inevitably stamp all human experience with anxiety. The lover's predicament on the urn is non-human in two senses: it is godlike in its perfection, it is also petrified and lifeless in its immobility: the urn is with "marble" men overwrought. If there is one conclusion that might be inferred (but I hasten to add that it should not) from Keats's treatment of the love-theme in his ode, it is that Beauty is not Truth, that is, if we take "Truth" to have any connection with the actual.

The third stanza, however, is only the end of the *first* episode in Keats's search for the meaning of art to life. Its last three lines are final with regard to the love-theme, but in another respect they are transitional. The poet has built up a concentrated picture of ideal love. With the last lines of stanza III he turns to the sufferings that necessarily accompany actual love; in the next stanza, he drops the love-theme entirely to concentrate on the theme of suffering and death, thus reaching a second stage in his poetic analysis of art. Although the second section consists of only one stanza, the beautiful artistic structure of the poem is not impaired because this one stanza repeats the whole pattern of the first section, beginning as it does with a series of unanswerable questions and ending on a note of deep melancholy. (There is modulation, of course, variety in this unity, and the melancholy at the end of stanza IV is different from, less harsh and more subdued than, the melancholy at the end of stanza III.)

Wasserman has made it clear that this stanza takes place in the mutable world, the world of time and space, in contrast with the first section, which deals with arrested change, with movement fixed into

[5] *The Parlement of Foules,* l. 130.

everlasting immobility. The three questions (who? whither? whence?) are the fundamental questions that can be asked about man, his origin, his destiny. In the dialectical development of the ode, a new aspect of art is now envisaged: art which is not beauty-centered, but truth-centered, in that it deals with the actual condition of man, the end and climax of which is death. The poet (as Wasserman has also pointed out) is no longer speaking of men that might be gods, but of ordinary folk from an ordinary town. This means that the two pictures on the urn are complementary: the first one deals with love and happiness and provides an idealized image of perfection which has little connection with the actual; the second deals with life as it is, its sufferings ("sacrifice"), its revolts ("lowing at the skies"), its sadness ("desolate"), its final absorption in the mystery of death ("not a soul . . . can e'er return"). The note of mystery is indeed conspicuous: the meaning of life, suffering, and death is impenetrable; not only do the questions asked remain unanswered, but the poet states that the little town will be silent for ever and that not a soul will ever return to tell *why* it is desolate (the word "why" completes the cycle of questions). Nevertheless, there is one thing in stanza IV which corresponds to the triumphant assertion of happiness in the first section: I mean the indirect intimation that, although the ultimate truth about human destiny is unknowable, nevertheless life has a meaning, which is essentially spiritual and religious ("sacrifice," "altar," "priest," "pious"): we remember that Keats had reconciled himself with the necessity of suffering, a month before, in April, 1819, while elaborating his philosophy of the world as "the vale of Soul-making."

The concluding lines of the ode have proved a matter of endless contention among critics. They have even been an obstacle to single-minded enjoyment because the apothegm pronounced by the urn sounds to some ears like a rather empty Platonic cliché. I think, however, that this gnomic utterance is more closely and more concretely related to the whole ode than is commonly realized.

The function of art, as exemplified in the way the urn affects Keats's mind, is twofold. To begin with, it "teases us out of thought." As Garrod has noted, the phrase is an echo from the *Epistle to John Hamilton Reynolds*. But the context is entirely different: it is no longer "things" which "tease us out of thought," but a work of art. In a way, this is a logical development from Keats's attitude in the *Epistle*, with regard to the two kinds of dreams, those that take their colors "from the Sunset" and those that "shadow our own Soul's daytime / In the dark void of Night." Since the latter reflect the world of actual experience, they must also tease us out of thought. But there is one conspicuous and all-important difference: in the *Epistle*, the poet suggests that

> Imagination brought
> Beyond its proper bound, yet still confin'd,—
> Lost in a sort of Purgatory blind,
> Cannot refer to any standard law
> Of either earth or heaven.                    (lines 78–82)

In the ode, art and imagination are no longer associated with "purgatory," but with "eternity." The total impression created by the latter poem is not one of puzzlement, but of wonder. In both cases the poet is teased out of thought, but the direction is different. The "things" in the *Epistle* refer to what Wordsworth had called

> the heavy and the weary weight
> Of all this unintelligible world [6]

while the urn is an object of mystery: this "cold" pastoral can express a love "for ever warm"; the "marble" men and maidens are "for ever panting"; although it is a "silent form," the urn is also a "historian" and a "friend to man," to whom it conveys a message of solace. Because of this *coincidentia oppositorum,* the work of art teases us out of thought in the same sense as eternity does.

The second function of art is formulated in the message itself. It is a custom, almost a rite, when discussing the *Ode on a Grecian Urn,* to quote Keats's famous dictum of November, 1817, about Adam's dream: "he awoke and found it truth." [7] Keats had certainly not recanted his notion that "what the Imagination seizes as Beauty must be truth—whether it existed before or not." [8] And it is this doctrine which is expressed in the first half of the urn's apothegm, "Beauty is truth," which, I venture to suggest, sums up in abstract terms the meaning of the first section of the poem: although the love scene is outside the actual conditions of human passion, it exhibits, through its sheer and immutable beauty, something of the quintessential truth of love. This is a Platonic truth: the beauty of art is due to the fact that art is the perfect embodiment of an Idea which, in actual life, can only manifest itself in imperfect forms owing to the limitations of human nature.

But the aphorism contains more than this favorite speculation of Keats's. The second half does not merely repeat in inverse order what the first half says. What it implies has been expressed by the author of *The Structure of Complex Words* in a typical flash of Empsonian insight:

[6] *Tintern Abbey,* ll. 39–40.
[7] *The Letters of John Keats,* ed. H. E. Rollins (Cambridge, Mass., 1958), I, 185.
[8] *Letters,* I, 184.

Keats was trying to work the disagreeables into the theory. It seemed to him, therefore, that the aphorism was *somehow* relevant to the parching tongue, the desolate streets, and the other woes of the generations not yet wasted. He, like his readers, I think, was puzzled by the remarks of the pot, and yet felt that they were very *nearly* intelligible and relevant.[9]

I do not know what evidence Empson could supply for his statement about Keats's understanding of his own poem. Much of what he says is, I am afraid, an aftermath of the once commonly held and utterly false notion that Romantic poetry is chiefly concerned with moods and attitudes and that we need not expect it to convey accurate or logical thoughts. Empson's italicized words, in the light of the foregoing analysis, seem to me completely out of place. But he is right in linking the artistic desolateness of stanza IV with the actual sorrow of stanza III and the woes of the last stanza, and in stating that "Keats was trying to work the disagreeables into the theory," that is, he was supplementing his theory of art as creation of ideal beauty with a theory of art as revelation of the beautiful in the actual.

The urn's pronouncement is thus seen as a fitting synthesis of the twofold dialectical movement of the poem: there is truth (in a somewhat Platonic sense) in the Elysian vision of the first scene; and there is beauty in the vision of ordinary life, suffering, and death described in the second scene. Whether the apothegm is to be considered as a pseudo-statement in the sense Richards gives to this word [10] depends upon the reader's own premises. (It would seem that any statement dealing with the non-measurable world can be construed as a pseudo-statement.) Keats, no doubt, meant it as a philosophical truth, although its relevance is strictly limited. Critics usually concentrate on the urn's dictum and overlook the last line and a half:

> that is all
> Ye know on earth, and all ye need to know.

One of them even pushed literal-mindedness so far as to observe that we need to know other things besides! But what if Keats used "all" in the sense of "the best," "the utmost," as in the phrase "That's all I can do"? Some such interpretation is suggested by the words "on earth," which clearly limit the range of applicability of the urn's statement. Art is not Eternity, but only an analogue of it. It is man's highest endeavor in this world because it actualizes the ideal and it makes perceptible the presence of the ideal in the actual. A Romantic

[9] W. Empson, *The Structure of Complex Words* (London, 1951), pp. 370–71.

[10] "A form of words which is justified entirely by its effect in releasing or organizing our impulses and attitudes." I. A. Richards, *Science and Poetry* (New York, 1926), pp. 58–59.

commonplace, one feels tempted to say; and it is true that it sums up in five words Hazlitt's conception of the "ideal" [11] as well as Coleridge's definition of the "symbol." [12] But by the time Keats wrote this ode, he had rediscovered the function of art for himself; he had come to feel it along his blood; it had been proved upon his pulse.

[11] W. Hazlitt, "Miscellaneous Essays on the Fine Arts: The Ideal," *Collected Works,* ed. A. R. Waller and A. Glover (London, 1902–4), IX, 429: "The *ideal* is the abstraction of any thing from all the circumstances that weaken its effect, or lessen our admiration of it. Or it is filling up the outline of truth or beauty existing in the mind, so as to leave nothing wanting or to desire further."

[12] S. T. Coleridge, "The Statesman's Manual," in *Biographia Literaria* (London, 1905), p. 322: "A symbol . . . is characterized . . . above all by the translucence of the eternal through and in the temporal."

# The *Ode on a Grecian Urn*

## *by Walter Jackson Bate*

Charles Brown's picture is unforgettable of Keats coming into the house from the grassplot after his morning's writing and quietly thrusting behind some books the loose scraps of paper that contained the *Ode to a Nightingale*—an action typical, Brown thought, of Keats's negligence about some of his shorter poems. But the further potentialities of the new form had plainly caught Keats's interest. For so consistently is the *Grecian Urn* given qualities the *Nightingale* lacked—though in the process it loses the personal urgency of the other ode—that whatever else entered into the writing of it, we find in it the concentration of a second attempt and of a conscious effort to learn from the first. The use of the song of the nightingale had been fortuitous. Some reflection may have preceded the choice of the steadier symbol of the urn—a symbol that would permit closer focus and a more craftsmanlike exploration of its potentialities and limitations. In contrast to the rapid shifts of pace in the *Nightingale,* the *Grecian Urn,* like the *Ode on Melancholy,* reflects the leisurely and "peaceable" spirit in which he hoped to write these new poems. Finally, with a determined objectivity, the poet—so prominent in the other ode—is now kept as completely out of the poem as possible. It is in every way a more considered poem than the *Nightingale.* This is not to say that it is superior. For it achieves its success partly because it is more limited in what it tries to say.

The lyric debate implied throughout the *Ode on a Grecian Urn* (it is significantly an ode *on,* and not, like the *Nightingale,* an ode *to)* has grown in the most organic way from sympathies as selfless and committed as they are divided, though personal preoccupations are also obvious and inevitable. The most abbreviated catalogue is enough to remind us of the strength of one commitment: the sonnet on Chapman's Homer, and those on the Elgin Marbles; the general ideal of "intensity"; the relish in power caught momentarily in repose (the "Miltonic stationing"). He was still returning frequently to see the Elgin Marbles, and perhaps within recent months had made the tracing that still survives, in the Keats House in Rome, of the Sosibios Vase.[1] But another commitment, probably even stronger now, can be suggested by the phrase that so haunted him, "the Burden of the Mystery"; by remarks about Wordsworth's thinking more into the human heart than Milton; by the thought of the heart as a "hornbook" from which the mind, in a world of "uncertainties, Mysteries, doubts," tries to spell out experience. This commitment to remain honest to human reactions—to explore the heart with its questionings and doubts—sustains the second voice that interplays with that of the odal hymn; and it is one of the several considerations we forget when we concentrate on the two closing lines of the poem ("Beauty is truth . . .") as an unqualified credo either to embrace or attack.

But debate is by no means predicated at the start. The essence of the urn is its potentiality waiting to be fulfilled. Unlike the song of the nightingale, so independent of human needs, the very origin of the urn presupposed the hope that it would be rescued into full existence by some later "greeting of the Spirit." For the actual parentage of the urn was the forgotten artist working with marble. It was only afterwards left to be the "foster-child of silence and slow time," though it has taken on the character of its foster-parents: it has lasted so long, and depicts a world now dead. Throughout that long fostering it has become pledged as a "bride of quietness." But this virginal bride is "still unravish'd," either by the infidelity of speaking or by the marriage consummation with "quietness" itself.[2] Finally, it is already able within limits to "express" a "tale," all the "more sweetly" because, like those early Italian prints Keats had described to George in December, there is "left so much room for Imagination." Hence, in contrast to the *Nightingale*, where questions appear only at the

---

[1] From the *Musée Napoléon*, a four-volume collection of engravings of works of art pillaged by Napoleon. Keats probably saw it at Haydon's. Attempts continue to be made to determine a particular vase or urn that Keats may have had in mind when he wrote the ode. Especially with a poem so distinguished by its universality, one thinks of Keats's own remark, written not long before the *Grecian Urn*, that "They are very shallow people who take everything literal." In all probability he was thinking principally of the Elgin Marbles. But a large collection would hardly have given him the focus he now wanted, however ready he may have been two years before to write his two general sonnets on the Marbles. Together with the Sosibios Vase, the Townley Vase in the British Museum and especially the engravings of the Borghese Vase in the Louvre (see Sidney Colvin, *John Keats* [1920], p. 416) may have suggested the idea of an urn.

[2] "Still," as an adverb, intensifies the possibility that it may yet be "ravish'd." But the word may have been intended as an adjective and was first printed thus ("Thou still, unravish'd bride of quietness") in *Annals of the Fine Arts*, IV (1820), No. 15.

end, the pattern here is one in which they begin, from the first stanza, to interplay with direct address. Half playful, they still presuppose a partial confidence. They begin as a general musing about the possibility of an elusive story or meaning beyond the actual figures on the urn: "What leaf-fring'd legend haunts about thy shape / Of deities or mortals or of both . . . ?" But as the imagination becomes more closely caught, it begins irresistibly to particularize, both in its own contribution or "greeting" and in its hope for response:

> What men or gods are these? What maidens loth?
> What mad pursuit? What struggle to escape?
> What pipes and timbrels? What wild ecstasy?

The eager questions, beginning to accumulate in rising empathy, are dismissed. Any communication from the urn must come otherwise, "to the spirit." In this withdrawal from question, the fact of the urn's silence in ordinary human terms is not only accepted but affirmed and even, for the moment, preferred:

> Heard melodies are sweet, but those unheard
> Are sweeter; therefore, ye soft pipes, play on;
> Not to the sensual ear, but, more endear'd,
> Pipe to the spirit ditties of no tone.

If a legend or hoped-for meaning "haunts about" the urn, then the imagination must do the same—"content with half-knowledge" and without "irritable reaching" after certitude. The approach now, therefore, is meditative. The poet simply addresses the figures without seeking to identify them. He adopts, in other words, the conventional romantic form of the *ut pictura poesis* tradition, in which the poet contemplates the work of art, often while directly addressing it, and derives from it a subject for meditation; and the theme of this meditation—in a sense the theme of all Keats's odes except *Psyche*—is that of process, and either the acceptance of it, or the hope to escape from it, or both in dramatic interplay with each other:

> Fair youth, beneath the trees, thou canst not leave
> Thy song, nor ever can those trees be bare;
> Bold Lover, never, never canst thou kiss,
> Though winning near the goal—yet, do not grieve;
> She cannot fade, though thou hast not thy bliss,
> For ever wilt thou love, and she be fair!

Yet if the questions that close the first stanza have been dismissed, the claims and frustrations of human needs have begun gently to reappear in another guise, preparing to become more assertive. They reappear, ironically, in the very act of approaching the urn not with impossible questions but with a meditative justice and delight that will acknowledge its unique character, its freedom both from process and from the distresses of the directly personal. Nor is freedom from process confined solely to freedom from physical change. The "enjoying of the Spring," as Keats had written in the lines on *Fancy,* fades just as inevitably as the actual "blossoming"; the ripeness of autumn ultimately "cloys"; the most beautiful eye will soon "weary"; nor is there any "voice, however soft," that "one would hear too oft."

But to acknowledge is partly to define or distinguish, and thus, by implication, to separate. At the very height of the acknowledgment (the beginning of the third or central stanza, in the latter part of which the ode makes its turn) we have the nostalgia of the outsider:

> Ah, happy, happy boughs! that cannot shed
>> Your leaves, nor ever bid the Spring adieu;
> And, happy melodist, unwearièd,
>> For ever piping songs for ever new.

In attempting to approach the urn in its own terms, the imagination has been led at the same time to separate itself—or the situation of man generally—still further from the urn. The result is the sudden release, in the middle of the third stanza, of diverse feelings shifting into each other but still fundamentally in opposition. Sympathy divides. In part it begins to desert the urn for the painful world of process, of which the urn is oblivious; and envy, incompatible with complete sympathy, follows. Yet the separation is not one-sided—there are at least two sides to any boundary—and no possible fulfillment exists for the figures on the urn apart from what the responsive mind can give them. As one sympathy withdraws from the urn, another seeks to redress the balance not merely by responding but by bestowing: love, in these frozen figures forever poised, is not only perennially young but "For ever warm" and even "For ever panting." Hence also the peculiar excess of exclamation in which a hastening reassurance and its opposite, nostalgic envy, equally join. As in the fourth stanza of the *Nightingale,* where the poem made its turn, there is a sense of strain. The repetitions there ("Away! away! for I will fly to thee") are matched by repetitions here that are possibly as urgent and certainly as helpless: the five "for ever's," and "More happy love! more happy, happy love!" As the stanza closes, the wrestle of feelings subsides into what appears to be an oversimple contrast:

> All breathing human passion far above,
>> That leaves a heart high-sorrowful and cloy'd,
>> A burning forehead, and a parching tongue.

But more is being deprived the figures on the urn than is bestowed.
They are now conceived negatively, through what they lack; and in
only the weak final line does their lack suggest much advantage.
"All breathing human passion" is a weighted phrase: "above," half
ironic, loses its evaluative force and begins to connote unawareness.
"Cloy'd" at least implies fulfillment. Finally a "heart high-sorrowful"
is able to experience the mystery of sorrow for which Keats, in the
revised *Hyperion,* was soon to find an image in the countenance of
Moneta.

\*   \*   \*

The second and especially the third stanzas have been a digression.
We have only to apply the simple test of omitting them both, or else
the third alone, and we find that what remains will still make a
complete poem, though admittedly less rich. On the other hand, if
we keep all the others and omit the fourth, or if we simply glance at
the close of the third and the opening of the fifth, we can see that
there would be no transition at all and that, in the third stanza,
Keats has found himself moving away from the principal feelings that
the urn at first suggested to him: a receptive delight in its permanence
of form, its mystery and inscrutability.

Hence the primary function of the fourth stanza is to return more
concretely to the Grecian urn and to some of the feelings that were
present at the start. As it does so, we find a result similar to what happens in the fifth stanza of the *Nightingale.* Each of these stanzas is
preceded by an impasse: an overeager, subjective, and finally frustrated empathy has tried to make the symbol carry more than it can,
and to use it in a massive protest against limitation or finitude, although that protest is itself divided. In each case the attempt to go
beyond the possibilities of both symbol and imaginative identification is finally abandoned; the approach is resumed in a more subdued
key; and then, paradoxically, a genuine empathy suddenly results.
Freed from the strain of taking the figures on the urn as literally alive,
the mind is able to develop if not to complete the suggestions offered
by them. The "imagination projecting itself into certain situations
. . . working up its imaginary feelings to the height of reality"—to
use the remark Keats had enthusiastically quoted from Hazlitt—is
gently transferred from the figures themselves to the world of which
they remain an emblem or representative. The references to them
become general: a "mysterious priest," a "heifer," "this folk." The
"green altar" to which they are going is not even shown on the white
urn, nor is the "little town," the location of which is unknown:

Who are these coming to the sacrifice?
  To what green altar, O mysterious priest,
Lead'st thou that heifer lowing at the skies,
    And all her silken flanks with garlands drest?
What little town by river or sea-shore,
    Or mountain-built with peaceful citadel,
      Is emptied of this folk, this pious morn?
And, little town, thy streets for evermore
    Will silent be; and not a soul to tell
      Why thou art desolate, can e'er return.

It is not simply because the figures are forever imprisoned on the urn that no one can ever return to the empty town but because the actual inhabitants disappeared in the remote past—a past from which no one remains except as figures on an urn or in other works of art.

As the mind has turned to the thought of the remote, forgotten life beyond the urn, the figures on it have become reduced to a stylized "brede" of "marble men and maidens"; and, as at the beginning of the poem, it is the urn as a whole that is now addressed. But in contrast to the beginning, where it had been approached as a possible "historian" that might reveal a "legend" of "deities or mortals," it is now acknowledged as only a "shape," or "form":

O Attic shape! Fair attitude! with brede
  Of marble men and maidens overwrought,
With forest branches and the trodden weed;
  Thou, silent form, dost tease us out of thought
As doth eternity.

The perennially disputed close of the poem then follows. The focus of the dispute is the final two lines, discussion of which already fills a small book of critical essays. The principal difficulties have been three, one of which has been almost completely resolved and another of which is largely of our own making. First, the abstractions "beauty" and "truth" are forced to carry the heavy, subjective load of meaning that Keats habitually gives them in his rapidly written letters. In his poetry, however, he tends to use abstractions of this sort sparingly and far less subjectively. Second, he was probably too ill to oversee the publication of the 1820 volume, where the lines were printed:

"Beauty is truth, truth beauty,"—that is all
  Ye know on earth, and all ye need to know.

Hence it was long assumed that the final remark is the poet's own personal comment on the aphorism, either as a consoling admonition to his fellow human beings (addressed as "ye" though he has been speaking in terms of "us" and "other woe / Than ours") or else as a congratulatory bow to the figures on the urn (though the whole burden of the stanza is what the urn, as a "friend," is offering to man). The texts of the transcripts make it plain that the entire two lines are meant as the message or reassurance to man from the urn, without intrusion by the poet.[8] Third, partly for these reasons, partly because of the aphoristic character of the final lines, they are constantly being separated not only from the context of the poem but even from the sentence in which they occur, and the efforts to put them back into their context only increase the concentrated focus on these innocent words. Perhaps the modern critical irritability with the phrasing would be less sharp if the Victorians themselves had not so frequently isolated the lines from their context and quoted them enthusiastically as what I. A. Richards calls a "pseudo-statement." Nothing so quickly arouses critical opposition as what we consider to be unthinking approval, though our irritabilities are in danger of becoming more concerned with replying to enthusiasms than with the full nature of the object in question. The spread of twentieth-century dissatisfaction may be typified by writers as diverse as Sir Arthur Quiller-Couch and T. S. Eliot. Quiller-Couch regards the lines as "a vague observation—to anyone whom life has taught to face facts . . . actually an *uneducated* conclusion, albeit most pardonable in one so young and ardent." Eliot, far more receptive, still finds the close a "blemish" or at least "grammatically meaningless."[4]

\*     \*     \*

[8] Fully discussed by A. Whitley, *KSMB*, No. 5 (1953), 1–3, and J. Stillinger, *PMLA*, LXXIII (1958), 447–48. All four transcripts (those of George Keats, Brown, Woodhouse, and Dilke) lack a full stop after "truth beauty," lack quotation marks, and by dashes break the final lines not into two parts but into three. That of Dilke is typical: "Beauty is truth,—truth beauty,—that is all . . . ."

[4] Eliot is taking issue with I. A. Richards, who, in discussing "pseudo-statements," speaks of those who misread the close of the *Grecian Urn* and "swallow 'Beauty is Truth, truth beauty . . . ,' as the quintessence of an aesthetic philosophy, not as the expression of a certain blend of feelings" (*Practical Criticism* [1929], pp. 186–87). Eliot goes on: "I am at first inclined to agree with [Richards]. . . . But on re-reading the whole Ode, this line strikes me as a serious blemish on a beautiful poem, and the reason must be either that I fail to understand it, or that it is a statement which is untrue. And I suppose that Keats meant something by it, however remote his truth and his beauty may have been from these words in ordinary use. And I am sure that he would have repudiated any explanation of the line which called it a pseudo-statement. . . . The statement of Keats seems to me meaningless: or perhaps the fact that it is grammatically meaningless conceals another meaning from me." "Dante," *Selected Essays* (1932), pp. 230–31.

The full sentence of the close is as follows:

Cold Pastoral!
When old age shall this generation waste,
Thou shalt remain, in midst of other woe
Than ours, a friend to man, to whom thou say'st,
"Beauty is truth, truth beauty,—that is all
Ye know on earth, and all ye need to know."

The final two lines are in the vein of the inscriptions on Greek monuments addressed to the passing stranger. The elusive message is meant to be that of the urn, not of the poet speaking for himself. In even the most spontaneous letters of a year and a half before (and we are significantly forced to go back that far in order to find remarks at all analogous), Keats never comes close to anything as bald as the simple equation of these two abstractions, "beauty" and "truth," that he permits the urn to make here (least of all does he advance anything seriously comparable to the words that follow). Not that those earlier remarks of Keats are irrelevant, as the purist would have it. They at least suggest something of the general premise involved in the urn's message. This very general premise, as far as Keats's own personal thinking is concerned, is that the "greeting of the Spirit" is itself as much a part of nature, or reality, as is its object. In the act of conception, with the resulting harmony ("beauty," "intensity") of the greeting mind and its object, we have a fresh achievement altogether within nature: a "truth—whether it existed before or not" in which reality has awakened further into awareness.

More specifically, the poem is ending with the assumption (which may not be completely justified) that the expression has been prepared for: that the urn maintains decorum—to use the classical term—by an expression dramatically appropriate to the character it has itself exemplified, the character of a work of art of a particular kind. Persisting through time, it itself remains ready to come alive ("wholly exist") as music on the printed page becomes alive when the inked notes are scanned and interpreted by some later imagination. The "spiritual," as Keats had written in his dramatic review for the *Champion* after he went to see Edmund Kean, "is felt when the very letters and points of charactered language show like the hieroglyphics of beauty"; and while these "mysterious signs" rise into life and meaning, we ourselves, approaching them from another age, begin to participate with them in a kind of "immortal free-masonry." Something of this experience is offered by the urn as a possibility. As such it will "remain, in midst of other woe / Than ours, a friend to man." So Milton, as Keats wrote earlier, continues even "since his death" to serve as "an active friend to Man." The thought is similar to that in the rondeau Keats had written in December ("Bards of passion and of mirth"). In addition to any Elysium where they may now be, the great poets of the past have also left souls behind to "Teach us, here, the way to find" them. Never slumbering, "never cloying," they continue to "speak / To mortals, of their little week."

Even so, the special and restricted character of the urn is stressed before its inscriptional message is permitted. Qualification is gradually built into the last two stanzas and particularly the closing sentence. Very much a part of the "truth" of human experience is the fact that every generation that views the urn is in the process of wasting, and living "in the midst of other woe / Than ours." Aloof from the brevity and sharp claims of human life, the urn is not only freer but also more limited: freer to advance the message it does in a way that no human being could confidently do, and yet, as a work of art, limited to the realm in which its message applies. The message is like itself: "teasing," perpetually available for certain valuable human experiences, and altogether oblivious of others—a message strictly applicable only to its own confined nature, in which beauty is not "a truth" (and it is the phrase "a truth" that Keats so commonly uses) but simply "truth" and is all that it itself knows or needs to know. But it is not all that man knows or needs to know: "how then are Souls to be made . . . but by the medium of a world like this? . . . Do you not see how necessary a World of Pains and troubles is to school an Intelligence and make it a soul?" The inanimate character of the urn is emphasized at the start of the final sentence as at no other point in the poem—"Cold Pastoral!" The message is that of a "shape," a "form," above all an "attitude," with the inevitable restrictions that this involves. Nor do we even receive it until this "shape" is first able to "tease us out of thought."

The word "attitude" is indeed of the essence of the poem's conclusion, and helpful to recall when we are tempted to concentrate on the last two lines as a subjective intrusion on the part of the poet, either directly or as a form of ventriloquism. It is also salutary to bear in mind Keats's robust realism, his sense of proportion and ready humor that apply as much to himself as to anything else. Like the Victorians, we are tempted to approach the great odes of April and May with more solemnity (which we too often equate with sincerity) than their creator ever thought it desirable or found it possible to sustain. We are willing to grant abstractly that his humor was irrepressible on even the most serious occasions. Struggling to understand the differences between the great poetry of the past and the challenge of the future, and only too aware of his own inadequacy, he could write movingly of the "Burden of the Mystery" and the "Chamber of Maiden-Thought," and yet at the same time he could play with the picture of himself creating a "rat-trap," with these two large demands (and with them the figures of Milton and Wordsworth) looming on each side. Forced by illness to return from the hopeful walking trip through the north, encountering the dying Tom, the hostile reviews, the serious effort of the next large poem, he could squirm comfortably on a cushioned chair when he reached Hampstead, look up with a tired grin, and say: "Bless thee, Bottom: bless thee! thou art translated." But when we come to the impassioned odes, we feel that we are dealing with a very different Keats. Yet he could finish writing out the ambitious *Ode to Psyche* with a flourish impossible to imagine from Wordsworth or Shelley or from any number of other poets: "Here endethe yᵉ Ode to Psyche." And not long before he wrote the *Grecian Urn* he could tell his sister that he was going to buy her some paste gems and seals at Tassie's shop, like the one he used as a seal for his own letters, and then ask her whether she wanted "heads of great Men such as Shakespeare, Milton &c—or fancy pieces of Art; such as Fame, Adonis &c—those gentry you read of at the end of the English Dictionary." "Fancy pieces of Art," with figures on them: what is the Grecian Urn? And "those gentry" one finds at the end of the dictionary include the characters not only of the embarrassing *Endymion* but of the great new effort, *Hyperion*. So on April 30, when Keats is finishing his long letter to George, the previous part of which closes with the pages about the "Vale of Soul-Making" and the human heart as the primer or "hornbook" to the mind. He has a few minutes to kill while he waits for Brown to finish copying some of his recent sonnets so that he himself can include them and the *Ode to Psyche* in his letter. In this vacant moment Keats starts an extemporaneous sonnet *On Fame* ("How fever'd is the man") which, within a line or two, turns to something rather different from what the title implies. It turns to man's general inability to accept his mortal, finite condition "with temperate blood," and to the tendency of the heart, through this self-defeating protest and anxiety, to "spoil" the very experiences possible to us as living, conscious creatures. Keats was completely aware of his own state of mind. With self-amusement, he heads the sonnet with a motto—firmly underlined—that could apply not only to the odes, to which he now turned, but also to the strange, brisk *Lamia* that follows them:

> *You cannot eat your cake and have it too*
> Proverb.

# Affirmation of Process in
## *Ode on Melancholy* and *To Autumn*

### *by David Perkins*

Even if we "imagine . . . happiness carried to an extreme," an un-mingled earthly bliss, "what must it end in?—Death—and who could in such a case bear with death—the whole troubles of life which are now frittered away in a series of years, would the[n] be accumulated for the last days of a being who instead of hailing its approach, would leave this world as Eve left Paradise." On the other hand, there is no likelihood of the world becoming such a paradise:

> The point at which Man may arrive is as far as the paralel state in inanimate nature and no further—For instance suppose a rose to have sensation, it blooms on a beautiful morning it enjoys itself—but there comes a cold wind, a hot sun—it cannot escape it, it cannot destroy its annoyances—they are as native to the world as itself; no more can man be happy in spite, the world[l]y elements will prey upon his nature.

Nothing is more implicit in the poetry of May to September, 1819, than this realization of the inevitability of suffering in a world of proc-ess. With this realization, the poet must seek some emotional accept-ance of life as it really is. The conception of the world as a "vale of Soul-making" is one such effort; for, continuing the letter already quoted, Keats wrote, "There may be intelligences or sparks of the di-vinity in millions—but they are not Souls . . . till they acquire iden-tities, till each one is personally itself. I[n]telligences are atoms of perception . . . how then are Souls to be made . . . but by the me-dium of a world like this? . . . Do you not see how necessary a World of Pains and troubles is to school an Intelligence and make it a soul?" [1] With the exception of such brief moods and fleeting intui-

---

[1] *The Letters of John Keats,* ed. H. E. Rollins (Cambridge, Mass., 1958), II, 101–2.

tions, however, Keats does not find any securely felt attitude. Perhaps he did not live long enough. But he did occasionally assert that man must turn to the concrete, experiencing it as fully as possible. This, indeed, is the theme of the *Ode on Melancholy* and *To Autumn*.

To discuss these odes together is to depart once again from the order of composition, but in this brief six months chronological development is less important than the one nexus of doubt from which all of the poems emerge. For if the transcendental idealism serenely expressed in the *Ode to Psyche* marks one extreme position in the self-debate waged from April to September in 1819, *Melancholy* and *To Autumn* stand at the antithetical pole. The three odes indicate the opposing boundaries and range of Keats's mature speculation. None of Keats's lyrics can be regarded as a settlement or resolution of the central uncertainties, and *To Autumn* and *Melancholy* are not exceptions. They are momentary affirmations, but, as with the other odes, the attitudes they express were deep-seated and persistent, and had any final summing up been achieved, these attitudes would also have been represented. In the background of these two odes, though not directly present in them, stands, first of all, Keats's own skeptical, questioning frame of mind which blocked a commitment to vision in the manner of Shelley or Blake. Secondly, there is the analysis of visionary experience worked out in the lyric and narrative poems of this period, leading Keats in the *Nightingale, Lamia,* and *The Fall of Hyperion* to suggest that the appeal of dreams may be deadly to the dreamer. And finally, there is the moral concern which results in a suspicion that to seek a subjective escape is unworthy or even contemptible. The harsh adjective is justified by the rigor of Apollonius, who speaks for one side of Keats, and by the self-condemnation voiced through Moneta.

*To Autumn* and *Melancholy* are not twin examples. *Melancholy* is rather an anticipation, an earlier exploration of what the flawless ode of four months later so triumphantly embodies. Here, in *Melancholy*, as in other poems, the paradise or haven man might desire would be to experience an immortal intensity in an ecstasy of unmixed pleasure. But among the general themes of the ode are the inevitability of process and the impossibility of what Keats elsewhere calls a "pure wine / Of happiness." To experience fully inevitably means to know pain or melancholy as well as pleasure. In fact, Melancholy has her "sovran shrine," is most to be felt, in precisely those experiences which are also most happy.

As we have seen, the desire for an immortal fulfillment has as its corollary the wish to escape from process. The very symbols which express the movement into the desired state of mind—wine or death in the *Ode to a Nightingale,* for example—become, if the movement is frustrated, symbols of non-experiencing. This theme appears, with more sober colorings, in *La Belle Dame sans Merci*, and also in *Lamia*, where the blocked attempt to rise into a visionary fulfillment really becomes a descent into oblivion. Translating these symbolic apprehensions into the language of exposition, one can see that they rise from the undeniable facts of psychological experience. A persistent habit of envisioning happy situations remote from present, actual circumstances naturally indicates a radical dissatisfaction with things as they are. If the dream or vision grounds itself in impossibility, fact will intrude, spoiling the satisfactions of the dream. In such a case, the alternative to an acceptance of things as they are would be an unconscious endeavor not to perceive or experience, a deadening of sensibility and awareness. At the beginning of the *Ode on Melancholy* the poet may be speaking to the man of "pale forehead"—the "pale warriors" of *La Belle Dame* who, like himself, have been unable to retain the satisfactions of vision—and urging that he should not take the downward course to oblivion ("go not to Lethe"). Thus many of the symbols usually associated with the flight into vision—the wine, the rosary of the religious aspirer, death and Psyche—are here indiscriminately lumped together and marshaled under the heading of Lethe as symbols of forgetfulness, perhaps suggesting that the aspiration to a visionary haven has converted itself into a desire for unawareness.

It may seem, however, that this interpretation is suspiciously pat to the theme I have been tracing, and that it is not fully justified by what is said in the poem. Certainly one does not have to go outside the poem to read the first stanza:

> No, no, go not to Lethe, neither twist
> > Wolf's-bane, tight-rooted, for its poisonous wine;
> Nor suffer thy pale forehead to be kiss'd
> > By nightshade, ruby grape of Proserpine;
> Make not your rosary of yew-berries,
> > Nor let the beetle, nor the death-moth be
> > > Your mournful Psyche, nor the downy owl
> A partner in your sorrow's mysteries;
> > For shade to shade will come too drowsily,
> > And drown the wakeful anguish of the soul.

Lethe, the poisonous wine, nightshade, and the like are symbols of death or oblivion in their own right. Moreover, in the first stanza the "death-moth" as a mournful Psyche, the "rosary of yew-berries," or the poisonous wine are also approximate equivalents to the beetle or the downy owl. They are images associated with melancholy. In the case of the "melancholy fit," to turn to such images is to seek what harmonizes with the mood. But things are defined by contrast, and in a universe of melancholy, its essence can scarcely be comprehended or felt. Instead, the "wakeful" perceiving of the soul is drowned. Of course, all these symbols are subsumed by the question of how to take the melancholy fit; for exactly this state can either create a deadened sensitivity or else it can be turned into a sharpened awareness of the concrete. The problem is the human use of it. The answer is not to dodge the melancholy through oblivion, but to experience through it. Against the attitude of the "pale warriors" of *La Belle Dame,* the poem urges an unreserved and intense involvement in process. The wakefulness of the soul is to the highest degree prized, even though, in the state of melancholy, the intensity may become anguish. Hence such expressions in the first stanza as "poisonous wine," the "forehead . . . kiss'd / By nightshade," or the "mournful Psyche" may have a significance that goes beyond what has been mentioned. In the first place, the wine would be poisonous, the "death-moth" a "mournful Psyche," and the like, not only in a literal sense but also because they do suggest an escape, if only into oblivion, and such an escape would be destructive to any possibility of happiness. More than this, however, the phrases bring together opposites—wine and poison, kissing and death—and so prelude or anticipate an important theme in the poem.

The perception that melancholy dwells with Beauty is not, of course, a mere rhetorical toying with antithesis. Neither is it simply the sentimental "Dejection taken up for pleasure's sake," the "sweet desolation—balmy pain" so frequently found in romantic poetry.[2] As recent critics have noticed, the pleasure-pain paradox, the coalescing of joy and sorrow in a single experiencing, runs throughout much of Keats's poetry. In the early verse, perhaps, this attitude to the nature of experience usually appears more as a flourish than as a perception vitally felt. Thus when Keats writes of birds "warbling for very joy mellifluous sorrow," or of bees who "know there is richest juice in poison-flowers," one need not take the expression very seriously. But as he continued to write, Keats clarified and deepened the content of such phrases. In *Hyperion* Apollo, awaking from a dream, played his lyre, and

>            all the vast
> Unwearied ear of the whole universe
> Listen'd in pain and pleasure at the birth
> Of such new tuneful wonder;        (III, 64–67)

and in the *Ode to Psyche* Keats speaks of "branchèd thoughts new grown with pleasant pain." It is true that in this context Keats refers only to creative activity, but then such activity is itself a type or even a metaphor of intense involvement.

---

[2] Wordsworth, *The Prelude,* VI, 551; Keats, *I Stood Tip-toe,* line 162.

The second stanza begins with a metaphor of process:

> But when the melancholy fit shall fall
> Sudden from heaven like a weeping cloud,
> That fosters the droop-headed flowers all,
> And hides the green hill in an April shroud.

At first glance, one might wonder why the metaphor is elaborated, and whether the details relate to the over-all movement of the poem. But it at least suggests that the melancholy fit is not wholly undesirable. The "droop-headed flowers" have a grammatical relation only with the "cloud," but the implication may be that the poet can also be awakened by a melancholy fit, a notion entirely consistent with the theme of the poem. More than that, however, the metaphor defines the conditions of life in a world of process, and implies that melancholy is inevitably a part of it. The "weeping cloud . . . hides the green hill in an April shroud"—a paradoxical phrase since April is the season of budding, the direct antithesis to the shroud or death-time. But at the same time, the cloud, with its suggestion of a temporary death, "fosters the droop-headed flowers," and without it there could be no fulfillment. When the melancholy fit falls one should seek to know it as fully as possible, and at the same time to savor things through the perspective it offers. Hence one should turn to what arouses a massive response in any mood. The morning rose, the "rainbow of the salt sand-wave," the "globèd peonies," and the rich anger of the mistress are all images of fulfillment, of things declaring their identity, revealing their essential being or "inscape," to use Hopkins's word; and the empathic reaction to these things creates the "havens of intenseness" which man would like to preserve. But the fulfillment is evanescent. The rose is a morning rose, its future uncertain as the day proceeds. "Suppose a rose to have sensation," wrote Keats, "it blooms on a beautiful morning it enjoys itself—but there comes a cold wind, a hot sun." [3] The rainbow of the wave is even more fleeting, for it forms as the wave rises to its crest and breaks. The anger of the mistress, one presumes, is equally short-lived. Yet even though these are momentary and fleeting, one can still possess them wholly. One can "glut" sorrow on a rose, "feed deep" upon the eyes of the mistress, and these images, presenting the sense of sight in terms of taste, suggest the intensity of the empathic response. Similarly, as W. J. Bate and others have pointed out, the phrase "globèd peonies" suggests the hand cupping the flowers in a full relish of their identity. At the same time, such expressions as "glut," or "feed deep, deep" imply a prolonging of the experience as it occurs. To become glutted takes

[3] *Letters*, II, 101.

a while, and the reiteration of "deep" draws out the feeding. The word "emprison" has a similar force, bespeaking a desire to arrest and hold immobile the momentary intensity. Thus as I said earlier, while these lines suggest the evanescence of the fulfillment, they also express the paradox of empathy—the unawareness of time at the height of intense experience.

But because these beautiful objects quickly fade, to turn to them is also to nourish the melancholy fit, and the last stanza generalizes the theme. Previously the poet had implied that melancholy is not simply a fit or mood, but something inextricably present in human life and experience. Now it is recognized that melancholy "dwells with Beauty" because beauty must die, and with Joy that is ever "bidding adieu." In pleasure so intense that it is "nigh" or almost aching—an emotion which becomes not simply pleasure but the full reaction of the whole being—melancholy resides, just as while the "bee-mouth sips"—an intoxicating image of delicate and intense pleasure—the nectar turns to poison in the bee's body. The metaphor perfectly expresses pleasure and pain slipping into each other and becoming one complex reaction in the organic processes of mind. In the "temple of delight" is the "sovran shrine" of Melancholy. But only the man who experiences most fully, the man of "strenuous tongue" and "palate fine," tastes the sadness at the core of "Joy's grape." Thus *Lamia, The Fall of Hyperion,* and the *Ode on Melancholy* can be seen as extending and clarifying a mood or attitude implied in most of Keats's major poems of 1819. In human life moments of intense experience decay as inevitably as they grow, and happiness cannot be disengaged from sorrow. To abstract materials from concrete life and build a visionary home leads to delusion and disappointment, and the hope to find some visionary reconciliation with process may vanish before accumulated experience and awareness.

*       *       *

Of the ode *To Autumn,* Allen Tate has said that it "is a very nearly perfect piece of style but it has little to say," and this opinion seems to be widely held.[4] But within the framework of Keats's habitual symbols and general attitudes, the ode seems to me unusually significant. Even more than Keats's other odes, *To Autumn* is objective, oblique, and impersonal, carried scarcely at all by direct statement that involves the poet. Like that of the *Grecian Urn* or the *Nightingale,* its expression is concrete and symbolic, and as in these other odes, the symbol adopted had been previously established in Keats's poetry.

[4] "A Reading of Keats," *American Scholar,* XV (Spring 1946), 58.

Something has already been said about his use of the seasons. Generally it is rather conventional: spring is the time of budding, summer of fulfillment, and winter of death. The poem, *The Human Seasons* (March, 1818), is typical as it runs through the "four seasons in the mind of man." In spring, the period of "youthful thought," man's growing faculties take in "all beauty with an easy span." Summer is the time of "luxuriously" enjoying or ruminating what was culled in the spring. Man "has his winter too of pale misfeature, / Or else he would forgo his mortal nature." Autumn, coming between summer and winter, can be seen as the intensifying and prolonging of summer. In other words, autumn suggests precisely that lengthening out of fulfillment as its crest or climax which Keats had desired to find in the concrete world. So the poet, turning to the concrete, to process, can contemplate it with serenity.

Autumn, accordingly, is described as a season of "mellow fruitfulness." The sun is ripening or "maturing" the earth, "conspiring" to load the vines and bend the apple trees, to "swell the gourd, and plump the hazel shells." In such verbs as "load" and "bend" there is a sense of strain. The season fills "all fruit with ripeness to the core"; and these images of full, inward ripeness and of strain suggest that the maturing can go no further, that the fulfillment has reached its climax. Even the cells of the bees are "o'er-brimm'd." Yet the ripening continues, "budding more, / And still more, later flowers." The bees —and the reader only partially identifies himself with them—"think warm days will never cease." Thus through the imagery the poem suggests an intensity of fulfillment prolonged and almost seeming to be immortal. At the same time, however, there are indirect images of aging. For the sun is maturing—it is not only ripening things, but it is also growing older. So also, one presumes, is autumn itself, the "close bosom-friend" of the sun. Process is taking place, and the season is drawing to a close, however slowly and unnoticed.

The second stanza picks up and continues the imagery of arrested motion in the first. Autumn is here personified in a variety of attitudes; but the dominant image is of autumn as the harvester—and a harvester that is in a sense another reaper, death itself. Instead of harvesting, however, autumn is motionless, death being momentarily held off as the ripening still continues. First autumn appears "sitting careless on a granary floor." The granary is where the harvest would be stored, but autumn is not bringing in the grain. The assonance and alliteration of the line, "Thy hair soft-lifted by the winnowing wind," leads into the image of autumn "drows'd" or "asleep" on a "half-reap'd furrow"—again the harvest arrested—"while thy hook / Spares the next swath and all its twinèd flowers." Finally autumn is seen by a cider press where it watches "the last oozings hours by hours." This is one of the two images suggesting activity (the other being the gleaner with "laden head" crossing a brook), but the motion is so slow that the reader takes the cider press almost as a repetition of the "half-reap'd furrow." But, of course, these are the "last oozings," and the harvest is drawing to a close. The notion of death is present to emerge more nakedly in the third stanza.

As with the "rainbow of the salt sand-wave" or the nightingale "pouring forth" its soul, things reveal their essential being or identity most intensely at the moment of dying or readiness to die. So the last stanza begins with the one comment the poet offers in his own person: "Where are the songs of Spring?" In the *Ode on a Grecian Urn* the same contrast between spring and the close of process was felt:

> Ah, happy, happy boughs! that cannot shed
> Your leaves, nor ever bid the Spring adieu.

In the *Ode on a Grecian Urn* the contrast leads or permits the poet to rebel against process in the wish to hold the spring forever. This rebellion, however, is now explicitly denied—"Ay, where are they? / Think not of them, thou hast thy music too." There follows an image of the day, which, like autumn, is "soft-dying," and the death is accompanied by a fulfillment; for as it dies the day blooms or flowers ("While barrèd clouds bloom the soft-dying day," and "touch the stubble-plains" with the warm color of the rose). The stanza proceeds with images of death or withdrawal, and of song, and the songs are a funeral dirge for the dying year. The "small gnats mourn" in a "wailful choir"; the wind "lives or dies"; "full-grown lambs loud bleat"; "hedge-crickets sing"; the "redbreast whistles"; and the swallows which are gathering for departure "twitter in the skies." At the same time the repeated suggestions of gentleness or softness—"small gnats," "light wind," "lambs," "treble soft," "twitter"—suffuse the stanza with a tone of tenderness; and the objectivity of the last few lines suggests an acceptance which includes even the fact of death. But death here is neither a pining for an "easeful" escape nor is it an intensity, a blind, climactic outpouring and release analogous to the song of the nightingale. Rather it is recognized as something inwoven in the course of things, the condition and price of all fulfillment, having like the spring and summer of life its own distinctive character or "music" which is also to be prized and relished. In the last analysis, perhaps, the serenity and acceptance here expressed are aesthetic. The ode is, after all, a poem of contemplation. The symbol of autumn compels that attitude. The poet's own fears, ambitions, and passions are not directly engaged, and hence he can be relatively withdrawn. And because spring is also subsumed in the context, he can seem to suggest that life in all its stages has a certain identity and beauty which man can appreciate by disengaging his own ego. Thus the symbol permits, and the poem as a whole expresses, an emotional reconciliation to the human experience of process.

# The Ode *To Autumn*

## *by Harold Bloom*

*To Autumn* is the subtlest and most beautiful of all Keats's odes, and as close to perfection as any shorter poem in the English language. That is of course cliché, but it cannot be *demonstrated* too often (it is more frequently asserted than evidenced). The incredible richness of this ode is such that it will sustain many readings, and indeed will demand them. To paraphrase G. Wilson Knight, *To Autumn* is a round solidity casting shadows on the flat surfaces of our criticism; we need as many planes at as many angles as we can get.

I am studying Romantic argument in these pages, and the argument of *To Autumn* is largely implicit. The problem here is to externalize it without removing it from the poem's own context.

The Autumn of the first stanza is a process and a beneficent agricultural conspirer, plotting secretly with the sun to bring ripeness to a state of all. The stanza is aureate, Spenserian in the globed fullness of its style, replete with heavily accented, single-syllabled parts of speech. As process Autumn loads, blesses, bends, fills, swells, plumps, and sets budding. The only receptive consciousness of all this activity is that of the bees, who sip their aching pleasure nigh to such a glut that "they think warm days will never cease," for the honey of harvest pleasure has "o'er-brimm'd" their natural storehouses. The fullness of nature's own grace, her free and overwhelming gift of herself, unfallen, is the burden of this ripe stanza. There is only a slight, but vital premonitory shading: the *later* flowers have deceived the bees.

The first stanza is natural process; the remaining two stanzas are sensuous observation of the consequences of that process: first sights of the harvest in its final stages; then, post-harvest sounds, heralding the coming-on of winter. The sequence of the three stanzas then is pre-harvest ripeness, late-harvest repletion, and post-harvest natural music. The allocation of the senses is crucial: the late-harvest art is plastic and graphic; the art of millennium. The art past ripeness and harvest

"*The Ode* To Autumn." *From* The Visionary Company: A Reading of English Romantic Poetry *by Harold Bloom (Garden City, N.Y.: Doubleday & Company, Inc., 1961), pp. 421–25. Copyright © 1961 by Harold Bloom. Reprinted by permission of Doubleday & Company, Inc., and Faber & Faber Ltd.*

is the art of the ear, apocalyptic, the final harmonies of music and
poetry. Here Keats, like Shelley, is Wordsworth's pupil. In the *Intimations* ode the visible glory departed with the summer of the body; the
ear, far inland, could yet hear the immortal sea, and so brought the
eye back to the autumnal coloring of a sobered but deepened imagination. The same process of heightened autumnal vision is celebrated by
Shelley in the final stanzas of his *Hymn to Intellectual Beauty* and
*Ode to the West Wind.* A more serene triumph awaits the modification of Wordsworth's myth in the final stanza of *To Autumn.* The
very same movement from sight to sound to final sight may be traced
also in the Night the Ninth of Blake's *The Four Zoas,* where the
beauty of the harvest of Millennium yields to the clamor of Apocalypse, to be succeeded by a final beauty beyond harvest. The ultimate
literary archetype for all this Romantic tradition is of course Biblical.

As the second stanza of *To Autumn* opens, we see Autumn already
"amid" her store. The promised overabundance of the first stanza has
been fulfilled; the harvest plot has been successful, the blessing so
overflowing that nature's grace abounds. Autumn is no longer active
process, but a female overcome by the fragrance and soft exhaustion
of her own labor. She is passive, an embodiment of the earthly paradise, the place of repose, after the sexual and productive activity
hinted at by her having been "close bosom-friend of the maturing
sun." But she is also the peasant girl drunk with the odors and efforts
of gathering, winnowing, reaping, and gleaning. She sits *"careless"* on
the granary floor; the word is very rich. She is careless because there is
more to be stored, though she sits, and yet amid all the fresh abundance she can indeed be without care. But the wind, softly lifting her
hair, which *is* the unreaped grain, reminds us of the winnowing yet to
be done. Again, she lies on her "half-reap'd furrow sound asleep,
drows'd with the fume of poppies," late bee-deceiving flowers, which
in a sense deceive her also. But the poem celebrates her drowsiness
even as it gently chides her, for her hook, in *sparing* the next swath,
spares also its twined flowers.

The final four lines of the stanza take us to the very end of harvest,
the gleaner bearing her laden head so steadily as to suggest motionless-
ness even as she moves, which further suggests the running-down to
stasis of a process. Finally we are shown the girl patiently watching,
hours by hours, the meaningful sameness of the "cyder-press" with its
final oozings, the last wealth of complete process itself. With those
"hours by hours" we are ready for the music of time in the final stanza.
We begin with only the "stubble-plains," but even as they are seen to
have their own peculiar visual beauty, so we are able to say that the
songs of Spring have been replaced by a different but not a lesser music.

> Where are the songs of Spring? Ay, where are they?
>   Think not of them, thou hast thy music too,—
> While barred clouds bloom the soft-dying day,
>   And touch the stubble-plains with rosy hue;
> Then in a wailful choir the small gnats mourn
>   Among the river sallows, borne aloft
>     Or sinking as the light wind lives or dies;
> And full-grown lambs loud bleat from hilly bourn;
>   Hedge-crickets sing; and now with treble soft
> The red-breast whistles from a garden croft;
>   And gathering swallows twitter in the skies.

This stanza looks back to the concluding lines of Coleridge's *Frost at Midnight,* where we hear:

>                   the redbreast sit and sing
>   Betwixt the tufts of snow on the bare branch
>   Of mossy apple-tree, while the nigh thatch
>   Smokes in the sun-thaw

and also forward to the final stanza of Stevens' *Sunday Morning,* where:

>           at evening,
>   In the isolation of the sky,
>   Casual flocks of pigeons make
>   Ambiguous undulations as they sink
>   Downwards to darkness, on extended wings.

Coleridge is extolling the sweetness even of winter as it will present itself to the country-reared, still-infant Hartley. Stevens, possibly remembering Keats even as Keats may be remembering Coleridge, is offering an image of natural death as an imaginative finality, a human consummation to be wished, though not devoutly. Keats is doing both: praising the red-breast and winter's other singers, and finding in the predeparture twitterings of the gathering swallows an emblem of natural completion. Winter descends here as a man might hope to die, with a natural sweetness, a natural movement akin to the extended wings of Stevens' pigeons or the organizing songs of Keats's swallows as they gather together for flight beyond winter. The day dies soft in this great stanza; the late flowers and poppies of stanzas one and two are replaced by the barred clouds that bloom the twilight and touch the stubble-plains with rosy hue. And though the *small* gnats mourn in a wailful choir, the sound of their mourning is musically varied by the caprice of the *light* wind, as it lives or dies; the poet's touch itself is light here. A final music replaces the lightness of

the mourning. The "full-grown lambs" are now ready for their harvest, having completed their cycle. The "hedge-crickets" are heard
across the exhausted landscape; the winter singer, the "red-breast,"
adds his soft treble, and the departing birds, seeking another warmth,
close the poem, which has climaxed in an acceptance of process beyond the possibility of grief. The last seven lines are all sound; natural music so varied and intense as to preclude even natural lament.
We feel that we might be at the end of tragedy or epic, having read
only a short ode. Where the *Nightingale, Urn,* and *Melancholy* odes
left us with the contraries, *To Autumn* fulfills the promise of the *Ode
to Psyche*: to let the warm love in, to resolve contraries, because there
is no further need for progression.

# The Artistry of Keats: A Modern Tribute

## by Cleanth Brooks

Modern criticism is intimately bound up with the rediscovery of the poetry of John Donne and with a restatement of the virtues of metaphysical poetry. There have been bitter observations to the effect that modern criticism has been concerned only with those virtues and that it deliberately refuses to see any virtue elsewhere. The modern critic, so the charge runs, is on principle anti-Romantic. The charge is unfair, as an examination of the writings of the modern critics will speedily show. But in view of its alleged bias, it ought to be interesting to see what modern criticism has to say about the poetry of John Keats.

One point becomes immediately clear: John Keats is not one of the villains of modern criticism. Richard Fogle, in his recent defense of Keats and Shelley against the attack of the modern critics, found, when he came to Keats, comparatively little to confute. The last chapter of his book turns out to be quite simply a defense of Shelley. With the adequacy of that defense, I am not concerned here, though the differentiation that recent critics have made—consciously or unconsciously —between Keats and Shelley may have its own significance.

My second point is less obvious—or rather this second point is not so much a historical observation as a prophecy: the Keats of the Odes may well prove to be one of the heroes of modernist criticism. If the reader considers this to be hardly praise—as if Keats's merits had to wait upon their recognition by the critics of the present day—I am cheerfully ready to agree. There is a sense in which no critical system is finally important. One may concede this, and concede further that criticism itself is judged and validated by its ability to recognize the fact of great poetry (though *what* is great poetry, we must never forget, is determined by an act of criticism). But I repeat my concession: for my concern here is not to vindicate the modern critics but to pay tribute to the artistry of Keats.

"The Artistry of Keats: A Modern Tribute" by Cleanth Brooks. From The Major English Romantic Poets: A Symposium in Reappraisal, edited by Clarence D. Thorpe, Carlos Baker, and Bennett Weaver (Carbondale: Southern Illinois University Press, 1957), pp. 246–51. Copyright 1957 by Southern Illinois University Press. Reprinted by permission of the publisher.

T. S. Eliot, in an essay that has been important for the development of modern criticism, characterized Donne's poetry as revealing the intellect at the tips of the senses. "A thought to Donne was an experience. It modified his sensibility."

What is important in this statement is the assertion of an integration of intellect and emotion—not the fact that Eliot makes *intellect* his first term, *senses,* his second. In describing the later poetry of Keats, *senses* will inevitably be our primary term. Critics have always emphasized Keats's sensuousness. But the connection between the senses and the intellect is there, and in the great poems, it amounts to an integration. In view of the poetry of the Odes, one could just reverse Eliot's suggested image of the intellect extended to the very nerve ends: with Keats, the nerve ends maintain contact with the intellect itself.

Put in this way, the concept may not seem very helpful. Isn't every true poet possessed of quick senses which are duly related to a central nervous system? And besides, didn't Keats himself see in the intellect an obstacle to the life of the imagination, complaining that "the dull brain perplexes and retards"? Yet Keats values knowledge, and for Keats the intensity of experience is not a blind blotting out of consciousness but a means of attaining knowledge—though a knowledge which transcends that accorded to the dull brain. Keats cultivates— almost like a connoisseur—"the wakeful anguish of the soul." No phrase is more characteristic of Keats. He refuses to drug it into insensibility—even in the *Ode to a Nightingale* where the heartache begins as a "drowsy numbness." The soul insists upon remaining awake and trying to understand its anguish, and indeed using its anguish as a means to understanding itself.

The foregoing comments, however, will hardly serve to pin down the basic matter in question: the specific sense in which Keats may be said to integrate intellect and emotion in his poetry. Perhaps the best way into the matter is through consideration of the central themes of the Odes. Take the theme of joy in beauty and melancholy at the loss of beauty. Keats is concerned with "Beauty that must die" (*Melancholy*), with Beauty caught and fixed by art (*Urn*), with Beauty that is transitory, yet apparently immortal (*Nightingale*). Logic and the dull brain would have it that the nightingale, though felt by the hearer in the Ode to be an immortal bird, is simply another instance of Beauty that must die. The nightingale, to be sure, may be abstracted from the transitory world of nature by the process of art. It might, for example, have been pictured on the urn, along with the happy boughs or the heifer lowing at the skies, but its immortality in that case would be the heavily qualified immortality of the other objects that go to make up the "cold pastoral." And in its duller moments the brain might propose additional difficulties: if unheard melodies are actually sweeter than heard melodies, how can the heard music of the nightingale move as it does move the hearer in the Ode? There, it is a kind of ecstatic culmination.

Our best counsel is not to ignore tactfully the apparent intellectual inconsistencies. It is rather to pursue vigorously the dialectic of the poetry. If we do so, we shall find that Keats's thinking is as acute and as responsible as any other poetic thinking—that, indeed, the thinking-through-images has gone beyond—not fallen below—such logic as the dull brain can manage.

Consider a relatively easy example. Keats's "April shroud" in the *Ode on Melancholy* is as characteristic of Keats as Donne's more celebrated shroud is characteristic of Donne. First of all, it is an *April* shroud, and the associations of joy and fruitfulness clash sharply with the more somber associations of the grave clothes. But the phrase is not merely a showy but incidental flourish of rhetoric. The "weeping cloud" covers the "green hill" with an April shroud, and the descent of the cloud is used to describe the falling of the "melancholy fit." But such a description argues that the melancholy is fruitful as well as sad. It catches up the references to "droop-headed flowers" fostered by the rain, to the "globèd peonies," and finally by implication, to the mistress herself, ultimate type of April and fruitfulness. Moreover, the phrase "April shroud" is already preparing for the collocation of joy and melancholy. The two are indissolubly joined. In our mortal world, birth and death are necessary to each other, and the taste of joy's grape, to the finer palate, has in it the most exquisite bitterness of melancholy. The phrase "aching pleasure" (line 23) points toward the same conclusion. Is an aching intensity of pleasure, pleasurable at all? It is and it is not. In any case, such pleasure is aching for its fulfillment, which is its obliteration in the love-death—an anticipation of death itself.

In the *Ode to a Nightingale*, this doubleness of death receives the most brilliant treatment that Keats ever gave it. Death is a horrible dissolution and falling away, but it is also the climax of ecstasy. It is alienation and separation but it is also integration and fulfillment.

The bird was not born for death. It cannot *know* what man, whose thoughts are from the beginning filled with a consciousness of impending death, cannot refuse to know. Lacking man's foreknowledge, merged in nature, the bird can express the wholeness of nature and can, in the poet's mind, itself participate in the unwearied immortality of nature. Man's self-consciousness is at once man's glory and his curse. It cuts him off from nature but this very detachment from nature makes it possible for him to *see* nature as a total thing, harmonious and beautiful.

I have elsewhere dealt in detail with this poem. In this brief note

I have space for only one or two examples of the part separate words and images play in building up the dialectical structure of the poem.

In the fifth stanza, death is suggested: the darkness in which the flowers are invisible, among them the violets which are "fast fading" —and most resonant of all, there is the word *embalmèd*. Yet the imagined scene carries no overtones of sterility and coldness—no hint of "deadness." The "incense" is that of living flowers—the place is a place of growth and birth—of the "coming musk-rose," "mid-May's eldest child." The stanza looks forward to "Now more than ever seems it rich to die" in the following stanza, and helps to interpret it.

How different in tone are the references to death earlier in the poem —"Where palsy shakes a few, sad, last gray hairs"—or later, when the poem has come full circle, where the song of the bird is finally *"buried deep in the next valley-glades."*

Or consider a related theme as carried by the light-dark imagery of the poem and focused on the word *fade*. The speaker's desire is for a breaking down of the distinctions such as the dull brain interposes between man and nature. He would "fade away into the forest dim"; he would "Fade far away, dissolve, and quite forget" what he as man knows but what the bird has never known. The process of dissolution is suggested by the imagined movement away from the world of clear outlines and sharply drawn distinctions into a world of shadows and darkness. The nightingale sings in a plot of "shadows numberless." As he moves toward imaginative identification with the nightingale, he moves into a region of "verdurous glooms" and into the "embalmèd darkness." His fading into the forest dim is a merging of himself with the world of nature, but the price is death—felt as a rich consummation as he listens "darkling," but seen in its bleak and chilling aspect at the end of the Ode when the "plaintive anthem fades" and is "buried." He would fade into the bird's song, but at the end, it is the bird's song that fades away from him.

In the *Ode on a Grecian Urn*, attention is focused upon a different kind of immortality and a different conception of integrated wholeness. The nightingale—part of the world of becoming—though it will die, was "not born to die"—lives without consciousness of death. The figures on the urn were not born at all—are as dead as the deadest stone, and yet in a sense are alive as their flesh-and-blood counterparts cannot be alive. Their alienation from the process of becoming is the very means to the wholeness and fullness of being that they possess. The urn baffles the dull brain as the song of the nightingale baffles it: it teases us "out of thought."

Both nature and art, as Keats contemplates them in the Odes, insist upon the human predicament. Man is involved in nature and yet through his consciousness transcends nature. He cannot accept birth and death as inseparable parts of a total process without being reminded that he too is involved in the process, his very organs of perception and awareness "fastened to a dying animal," and if he would fix his vision of totality beyond the flux of change, it is only by some such act as that of freezing it in cold marble, itself lifeless. To immerse oneself in the flux of change is to forfeit knowledge of it. Immersion in nature is a dissolution of the self which ends in lack of consciousness: "To thy high requiem become a sod." To detach oneself from the process in pure contemplation ends in the contemplation of changeless but lifeless stone.

Keats, by the way, would not be in the least shocked by E. E. Cummings' lines that state: "A pretty girl that naked is / Is worth a million statues." The *Ode on a Grecian Urn,* so different in tone from Cummings' admirable little poem, has absorbed and digested into itself that, among other related notions. The Odes are tough-minded, not soft and self-indulgent or prettified or—as Cummings' Bowery tough would put it—fancy. They deal an even-handed justice between the claims for the pretty girl that naked is and for the marble maidens that embellish the urn.

I have studiously avoided using such terms as paradox and irony, not because I do not think that these terms fully apply, but because these terms have raised so much opposition among the lovers of Romantic poetry that I do not want to risk obscuring my point. It is the point that is important—not the terms as such. In the Odes there is an integration of intellect and emotion. Form *is* meaning. The thinking goes on through the images and receives its precise definition and qualification from the images.

This last generalization is a conclusion to which I, at least, have not come speedily or easily. I must apologize for past blunderings and misreadings, occasions on which I felt that Keats was confused or careless and that his images were used as mere surface decoration. But the blunders have turned out to be my own, not the poet's, and even Keats's apparently casual choice of a word has usually vindicated itself.

Is one to say, then, that Keats was a monster of prevision, carefully working out the intellectual ramifications of his poems, adjusting this image and that to the precise development of a preconceived intellectual scheme? Not at all, though in view of what we know of Keats's revisions, few will want to insist upon the hypothesis that he composed hastily and unthinkingly. But I have no theory to offer concerning Keats's psychology of composition. My case for the intricate coherency of the Odes is based upon the texts of the poems themselves. What I think we can say—and probably must say—is this: that the imagery, however spontaneously it may have come to Keats's mind, was shaped, consciously or unconsciously, by that mind to a precision that is beautifully exact. The poems seem to me inexhaustibly rich. Even if the sensuous detail was the conscious preoccupation of the poet, the detail as given is more than that: it teases us *into* thought—not into vague ruminations, but into amazingly precise and profound thinking about the nature of man. Donne could say "This ecstasy doth unperplex . . . and tell us what our souls are." Keats's celebrations of ecstasy are no mere swoonings: they "unperplex" us in the same fashion.

# PART TWO

# View Points

## Leonidas M. Jones: Ode to Psyche

Psyche symbolizes, of course, the soul in the old sense of the word, the sum total of the human consciousness. For Keats, we may be sure, a most important component of that consciousness was the imagination. In promising to worship Psyche, he was announcing his intention allegorically of becoming a psychological poet, of analysing the human soul, of glorifying the imagination, of studying the human mind in order to show how an awareness of its complexity could enrich human experience. . . .

It is especially appropriate that Keats chose Psyche as his object of worship, because for him the best means of approaching the immortal world was through the use of the most active ingredient of the human soul, the imagination. A simple belief in the old gods was no longer possible, but man was not therefore doomed to mere animality. He might still employ the imagination to break through the bounds of the mortal and finite. Psyche was an excellent symbol for the imagination as an instrument to bridge the gap between the mortal and immortal because she stood between both: she had been mortal and she became a goddess.

From "The 'Ode to Psyche': An Allegorical Introduction to Keats's Great Odes" by Leonidas M. Jones, Keats-Shelley Memorial Bulletin, IX (1958), 23. Reprinted by permission of the author and the editor of Keats-Shelley Memorial Bulletin.

## David Perkins: Ode to Psyche

The doubts suggested by the question "Surely I dreamt to-day, or did I see" have already been mentioned. There is also the word "fond" in the "fond believing lyre." It seems to hover between "affectionate" and the older meaning of "foolish" or "doting," suggesting a tenderness wishful and possibly indulgent. Again in the last stanza a reservation may be implied when Psyche is promised "all soft delight / That shadowy thought can win"; for with Keats delight is more usually

From The Quest for Permanence: The Symbolism of Wordsworth, Shelley, and Keats by David Perkins (Cambridge, Mass.: Harvard University Press, 1959), pp. 226–28. Copyright 1959 by the President and Fellows of Harvard College. Reprinted by permission of the publishers.

associated with particular, concrete experience than with what thought
—particularly "shadowy thought"—alone can give. Similarly the stars
that Fancy supplies are "without a name." This may imply merely
that they will be stars other than those we know, or it may more omi-
nously suggest that these stars lack concrete identity, just as with the
Grecian urn the poet asks "What men or gods are these" and gets—
and expects—no answer. One should also note that the paradise will
hold all that "the gardener Fancy e'er could feign," and the word
"feign" recalls the partial disillusion at the close of the *Ode to a
Nightingale*: "Adieu! the fancy cannot cheat so well / As she is fam'd
to do, deceiving elf." But most of all one wonders about the frank
recognition that the visionary poet must work subjectively, that because the poet worships Psyche in an unbelieving world, the worship
must be private. It can exist only in the mind, and even in "some untrodden region" of the mind, a place set apart and secluded where
other processes of cognition will not intrude. In other words, the visionary and the mortal worlds cannot be known simultaneously or in
juxtaposition, and, like Madeline withdrawing to dream in her chamber, the poet must protectively isolate the vision in order to enjoy it.
To the extent that he consecrates his own mind as a "shrine" to Psyche
he retreats from confronting "the agonies, the strife / Of human
hearts." The very clear recognition of this which the ode expresses
later became one reason for rejecting an openly visionary poetry. In
the ode itself, however, these implications seem to be more than acknowledged; they are welcomed, and the poet expresses a firm resolve
to protect his vision from the withering touch of actuality.

## Anthony Hecht: Ode to a Nightingale

The nightingale was heard long ago by all sorts and conditions of
people, reminding them of the generations past, and what could have
been more apt than the sound of that song to Ruth, who seems even
more remote to us (because of the quasi-real context of the Bible)
than the ancient days of emperor and clown. And more remote yet,
due to a general dubiety about their reality-status, are those "magic
casements, opening on the foam / Of perilous seas, in faery lands forlorn." Indeed, "forlorn" is the key word here, not only because it recalls the poet to his isolated self, but because it has to do with the
central problem of the whole poem: a reliance upon and confidence
in the powers of the imagination. The faery lands are forlorn precisely because nobody any longer believes in them. And on what

*From "Shades of Keats and Marvell" by Anthony Hecht, The Hudson Review,
XV, No. 1 (Spring 1962), 64–66. Reprinted by permission of The Hudson Review.*

grounds are we to claim that Ruth, or the emperor and clown are more real and worthy of belief, since it is only by an act of the imagination that we can apprehend them? And most important of all, if the faery lands were "merely" the perishable creations of imagination, now abandoned for want of belief in them, what confidence, if any, may we have in the reality of the imagination, including the experience the poet has just gone through? The degree of self-consciousness invoked by that one word, "forlorn," which tolls the poet back to his "sole self" is staggering as well as sudden. And this is by no means the only poem of Keats's in which this problem is made central and dramatic; in fact, it is one of his major themes. In the *Ode to Psyche* he laments that the goddess has "No shrine, no grove, no heat / Of pale-mouthed prophet dreaming," and goes on to say, "O brightest! though too late for antique vows, / Too, too late for the fond believing lyre. . . ." Nevertheless, he volunteers to be her priest, "and build a fane / In some untrodden region of my mind, / Where branchèd thoughts, new grown with pleasant pain, / Instead of pines shall murmur in the wind. . . ." It should be noticed, however, that in the Psyche Ode the problem is not fully faced because the continuity between the exterior and interior world is made so fragile and tenuous as not really to present a problem at all. It is, in its own mode, thoroughly successful, and has what may be the most breathlessly passionate ending of any poem in English. The Nightingale Ode, on the other hand, is busy making metaphysical inquiries about itself such as the Psyche Ode does not contemplate; and in my opinion this gives it a density and complexity which I must deny the other in spite of its indubitable beauty. The difference between the odes is precisely the difference between Psyche (goddess & mind) and a nightingale (symbol of art through suffering & a bird); in one case there is no need for the *facts* of the outside world to be acknowledged; but the bird starts off as a bird and must remain one, no matter how much mythical weight it is made to bear. Moreover, the fact that the Nightingale Ode ends irresolutely seems to me both dramatic and honest, and in no way to diminish its force and point. For the fact is that we are entitled to an unresolved doubt at the end. It is true, the claims that were made upon the "fancy" were extravagant; but the experience of the poet, up to a certain point, has undoubtedly been real enough, and it was almost entirely predicated on that "deceiving elf," the fancy. Almost, except for the bird-song. And that song, like this poem, is both "an ecstasy" and a "requiem." If the bird-song "fades" as the imagination fails, and if the poet is left in doubt about the reality of his present lonely circumstances as well as the reality of the ecstasy (which was a kind of token death), we are left with the paradox that the numbness, bewilderment and confusion which he so much desired at the beginning of the poem he now has in plenty, but finds it only distressing. And yet the paradox is not real, for like Marvell, he did not quite die, but was left only with the symptoms of death. And his despair, if that's what it is, arises from being "tolled back" as by a death-knell from the sovereign heights above the perilous seas. It is death to faery land, and a sudden vacant, non-ecstatic death to him. But it is death to the imagination only if the whole poem is called into question. There is no doubt that Keats does so call it, but I should think that he hoped it would offer its own uncompromising answer.

## F. W. Bateson: Ode on a Grecian Urn

The Urn, for one thing, is not a symbol in the sense in which the West Wind and Blake's Tiger and Keats's own Nightingale are symbols. There is no question here of an "objective correlative." The Urn really only provides an object lesson. By the use of analogies from the Urn Keats is able to make a number of points about the nature of poetry.

The Urn is introduced as comparable with but superior to poetry:

> Sylvan historian, who canst thus express
> A flowery tale more sweetly than our rhyme.

*Endymion,* it will be remembered, had opened with the claim that poetry provided "A flowery band to bind us to the earth." The Urn, then, can beat poetry at its own game. And what that game is is exemplified in the *motionless movement* of l. 9 of stanza I,

> What mad pursuit? What struggle to escape?

Stanza II elaborates the definition with examples of *soundless sound* ("ditties of no tone"), *stationary growth* ("Nor ever can those trees be bare"), and *timeless time* ("For ever wilt thou love, and she be fair"). Stanzas III and IV draw certain pathetic and whimsical corollaries, and stanza V sums up the paradox of poetry. As Coleridge, with whom Keats had walked across Hampstead Heath as recently as the previous April, had taught his contemporaries, poetry "reveals itself in the balance or reconcilement of opposite or discordant qualities." And Hazlitt, Keats's principal critical mentor, had made the same point even more clearly when he attributed to Shakespeare "the combination of

*From* English Poetry: A Critical Introduction *by F. W. Bateson, revised edn.* (New York: Barnes & Noble, Inc., 1966), pp. 152–54. Copyright 1966 by F. W. Bateson. Reprinted by permission of Barnes & Noble, Inc., and Longmans, Green & Co. Ltd.

the greatest extremes." "Shakespeare's imagination is rapid and devious. It unites the most opposite extremes." . . .

The much-debated "Beauty is truth, truth beauty" must be interpreted in this context. The Urn is a "Cold Pastoral"; that is to say, like pastoral poetry (the only sense the noun *pastoral* had in the nineteenth century), it is allegorical. Behind the particular unions of opposites depicted on the Urn (motion and immobility, growth and permanence, time and timelessness, etc.) a general synthetic principle is implied. This is the necessity for uniting Romanticism ("beauty") and realism ("truth"), the subconscious with the conscious mind, the feeling with the concept, poetry and philosophy. It is Keats's protest against the Romantic "split man." And the point of particular interest is Keats's *social* motive in propounding this generalization. The Urn is "a friend to man." The lesson that it teaches will be consolatory to the next generation as well as to Keats's. Indeed, compared to the need for psychological integration other social problems are of secondary importance:

> that is all
> Ye know on earth, and all ye need to know.

Keats oversimplified, of course, but to say, as Allen Tate has done, that stanza V "is an illicit commentary added by the poet to a 'meaning' which was symbolically complete at the end of the preceding stanza" is to miss Keats's point. Stanza IV had been a relapse into Romanticism. The "green altar," the "mysterious priest" and the "little town" were alluring invitations to reverie. But Keats was too honest to leave it at that. The *Ode to a Nightingale* had ended with the explicit admission that the "fancy" is a "cheat," and the *Grecian Urn* concludes with a similar repudiation. But this time it is a positive instead of a negative conclusion. There *is* no escape from the "woe" that "shall this generation waste," but the action of time can be confronted and seen in its proper proportions. To enable its readers to do this is the special function of poetry.

## Douglas Bush: Ode on a Grecian Urn

The great odes of the spring were variations on one theme, a theme complex enough as Keats consciously conceived it and further compli-

*From "Keats and His Ideas" by Douglas Bush, in* The Major English Romantic Poets: A Symposium in Reappraisal, *edited by Clarence D. Thorpe, Carlos Baker, and Bennett Weaver (Carbondale: Southern Illinois University Press, 1957), pp. 240–41. Copyright 1957 by Southern Illinois University Press. Reprinted by permission of the publisher.*

cated and intensified by his half-unconscious doubts of his own aesthetic resolution. The *Ode to Psyche* is devoid of explicit "ideas," except as its animating idea is the power of the imagination to preserve and transmute direct sensuous experience. That theme causes no conflict in *Psyche*; but conflict is central in the *Nightingale* and the *Grecian Urn*. In these two odes Keats feels not so much the joy of the imaginative experience as the painful antithesis between transient sensation and enduring art. He cannot wholly accept his own argument, because both his heart and his senses are divided. The power of the imagination, the immortality of art, offer no adequate recompense for either the fleeting joys or the inescapable pains of mortality. Keats's early desire to burst our mortal bars, to transcend the limitations of human understanding, becomes in the *Nightingale* the desire for death, the highest sensation, or an anguished awareness of the gulf between life and death. In the end the imagination cannot escape from oppressive actuality; far from attaining a vision of ultimate truth, it achieves only a momentary illusion.

In the *Grecian Urn*, the sensations evoked are almost wholly concerned with young love (the great fourth stanza is logically a digression), and again Keats cannot convince himself that love and beauty on marble are better than flesh-and-blood experience, however brief and unhappy that may be. It is the underlying lack of satisfaction that inspires the unrelated picture of the little town, for ever empty of humanity, a picture almost forced upon the poet, as it were, by his recognition of the negative side of his theme. But he overrides his emotional skepticism (though it comes up again in "Cold Pastoral"), and ends with the positive statement of his most famous "idea," a statement that has been much questioned on the score of both meaning and artistic propriety. The meaning (and the meaning of similar utterances in the letters) may be simpler than some of the explanations of it. In a world of inexplicable mystery and pain, the experience of beauty is the one sure revelation of reality; beauty lives in particulars, and these pass, but they attest a principle, a unity, behind them. And if beauty is reality, the converse is likewise true, that reality, the reality of intense human experience, of suffering, can also yield beauty, in itself and in art. This is central in the poet's creed, if not all explicit in this poem, yet the undercurrent here prevents the urn's assertion from being the Q.E.D. it is intended to be. If the *Grecian Urn* and the *Nightingale* rise above *Psyche* and *Melancholy*, the reason is not only their artistic superiority but the complexity of their unresolved tensions. They were begun, so to speak, by the poet of sensuous luxury, but were taken over by the poet who had learned on his pulses the knowledge given to Apollo and could not escape from it.

## M. H. Abrams: *Ode on a Grecian Urn*

"Beauty is truth, truth beauty" is not asserted by Keats, either as a statement or as a pseudo statement. The Grecian Urn, after remaining obdurately mute under a hail of questions, unexpectedly gives voice to this proposition near the end of the poem. In discussions of the problem of belief the significance of this obvious fact is often overlooked or minimized. Middleton Murry, for example, although he observes that the speaker is the Urn, goes on immediately to reconstruct the biographical occasion Keats himself had for such a comment, and then (like so many other critics) evolves an elaborate aesthetico-ontological theory to demonstrate that the statement is philosophically valid, and merits assent. For his part, I. A. Richards describes "Beauty is truth" as "the expression of a certain blend of feelings," and asks us to accept such emotive expressions without belief; and T. S. Eliot replies that he would be glad to do so, except that "the statement of Keats" seems to him so obtrusively meaningless that he finds the undertaking impossible.

There is also a second and more important speaker in the poem. The whole of the *Ode on a Grecian Urn*, in fact, consists of the utterance of this unnamed character, whose situation and actions we follow as he attends first to the whole, then to the sculptured parts, and again to the whole of the Urn; and who expresses in the process not only his perceptions, but his thoughts and feelings, and thereby discovers to us a determinate temperament. By a standard poetic device we accept without disbelief, he attributes to the Urn a statement about beauty and truth which is actually a thought that the Urn evokes in him. How we are to take the statement, therefore, depends not only on its status as an utterance, in that place, by the particular Urn, but beyond that as the penultimate stage, dramatically rendered, in the meditation of the lyric speaker himself.

Obviously the earlier part of the *Ode* by no means gives the Urn a character that would warrant either its profundity or its reliability as a moral philosopher. In the mixed attitudes of the lyric speaker toward the Urn the playfulness and the pity, which are no less evident than the envy and the admiration, imply a position of superior understanding:

> Bold lover, never, never canst thou kiss,
>   Though winning near the goal—yet, do not grieve;
>     She cannot fade, though thou hast not thy bliss . . . .

From "*Belief and the Suspension of Disbelief*" by M. H. Abrams, Literature and Belief: English Institute Essays, 1957, *edited by* M. H. Abrams (*New York: Columbia University Press, 1958*), *pp. 13–16. Copyright 1958 by Columbia University Press. Reprinted by permission of the publisher.*

The perfection represented on the Urn is the perdurability of the specious present, which escapes the "woe" of our mutable world only by surrendering any possibility of consummation and by trading grieving flesh for marble. The Urn, then, speaks from the limited perspective of a work of Grecian art; and it is from the larger viewpoint of this life, with its possibilities and its sorrows, that the lyric speaker has the last word, addressed to the figures on the Urn:

> That is all
> Ye know on earth, and all ye need to know.

The Urn has said, "Only the beautiful exists, and all that exists is beautiful"—but not, the speaker replies, in life, only in that sculptured Grecian world of noble simplicity where much that humanly matters is sacrificed for an enduring Now.

I entirely agree, then, with Professor Brooks in his explication of the *Ode,* that "Beauty is truth" is not meant "to compete with . . . scientific and philosophical generalizations," but is to be considered as a speech "in character" and "dramatically appropriate" to the Urn. I am uneasy, however, about his final reference to "the world-view, or 'philosophy,' or 'truth' of the poem as a whole." For the poem as a whole is equally an utterance by a dramatically presented speaker, and none of its statements is proffered for our endorsement as a philosophical generalization of unlimited scope. They are all, therefore, to be apprehended as histrionic elements which are "in character" and "dramatically appropriate," for their inherent interest as stages in the evolution of an artistically ordered, hence all the more emotionally effective, experience of a credible human being.

## Leonard Unger: To Autumn

It seems generally agreed that *To Autumn* is a rich and vivid description of nature, expertly achieved within a fairly intricate stanzaic pattern. The words are successfully descriptive (or evocative) in their phonetic qualities and rhythmical arrangement, as well as in their imagistic references. If we are familiar with Keats's other work, however, we can discover that the poem is not only rich in pictorial and sensuous details, but that it has a depth of meaning and a characteristic complexity of structure. *To Autumn* is allied especially to the odes on Melancholy, on a Grecian Urn, and to a Night-

*From "Keats and the Music of Autumn," The Man in the Name: Essays on the Experience of Poetry by Leonard Unger (Minneapolis: University of Minnesota Press, 1956), pp. 20–21. Copyright 1956 by the University of Minnesota. Reprinted by permission of the publisher.*

ingale. The four poems are various treatments presenting differing aspects of a single theme.

In so far as the theme is "stated" in any of the poems, it is most clearly stated in the *Ode on Melancholy*. In fact, if we want a general formulation of the theme, we need only quote the last stanza—especially these lines:

> Ay, in the very temple of Delight
> Veil'd Melancholy has her sovran shrine,
> Though seen of none save him whose strenuous tongue
> Can burst Joy's grape against his palate fine.

Keats was obviously preoccupied with the consideration that beauty and melancholy are closely related: true melancholy is to be found only in the fullness of living, in beauty, joy and delight, for these experiences make most poignant the passage of time, through which such experiences and then life itself must come to an end.

All this is clear enough in the *Ode on Melancholy*. There is, however, the implication that the relationship between beauty and melancholy works both ways. That is, either joy or sadness is most intensely felt when it is attended by a consciousness of the experience which is opposite and yet so closely related to it. The theme, then, is more complex and subtle than the aspect of it which appears on the surface in *Ode on Melancholy*. Other implications of the theme may be found throughout the four poems, which illuminate and clarify each other. This is not to say that the poems are merely repetitions of the same theme, which Keats had in mind before he wrote any of them. When we understand the poems we might find it more accurate to say that each is the exploration of a certain theme.

# Appendix:
## Who Says What to Whom at the End of
## Ode on a Grecian Urn?

Interpretation of the final lines of *Ode on a Grecian Urn* has frequently turned on the specific questions of who speaks the last thirteen words, and to whom. The textual evidence is inconclusive (see *PMLA*, LXXIII [1958], 447–48); each of the following versions has a claim to authority:

> Beauty is Truth,—Truth Beauty,—that is all
> Ye know on earth, and all ye need to know.
> > (consensus of four transcripts; capitalization varies)

> Beauty is Truth, Truth Beauty.—That is all
> Ye know on Earth, and all ye need to know.
> > (*Annals of the Fine Arts, for MDCCCXIX,*
> > publ. c. Jan., 1820)

> "Beauty is truth, truth beauty,"—that is all
> Ye know on earth, and all ye need to know.
> > (Keats's *Lamia* volume, publ. July, 1820)

No single explanation can satisfy the demands of text, grammar, dramatic consistency, and common sense. But critics do tend to stand on single explanations, and it may therefore be useful to summarize briefly the various possibilities, along with the objections usually raised against each.

(1) *Poet to reader:* The poet, commenting on the urn's "message," says "that is all / Ye know on earth, and all ye need to know" to the reader (and thereby to mankind generally). This is a common older interpretation which, like (2) and (3) below, is based at least initially on the *Lamia* volume's use of quotation marks to separate "Beauty . . . beauty" from the rest of the two lines. J. M. Murry, *Keats* (1955), pp. 210–26, is a typical proponent of the view. *Objections:* The reader and man have become "us" and "ours" in the final stanza; the poet's shift of address to "ye" would be both inconsistent and unprepared for (he has not earlier spoken directly to the reader/mankind). Then there is the question of meaning. At face value, the statement is false to everybody's experience of life—as one unsympathetic reader put it, "Beauty ain't truth and truth ain't beauty and you've got to know a helluva lot more than that on earth." (Critics of course have to go

past face value. Victor M. Hamm, *Explicator*, III [1945], item 56, paraphrases, "That is all you [anyone contemplating the urn] know about the urn, and all you need to know," and reads the lines as a reply to the unanswered questions posed in the first and fourth stanzas.)

The explanation by Earl Wasserman, *The Finer Tone* (1953), p. 60, should be included under this heading: the poet's words to the reader, "that . . . know," refer not only to the urn's "message" but to the three lines preceding—"When old age . . . ." An additional objection here is the obscurity of reference, since few readers, unaided, would grasp the intended scope of "that."

(2) *Poet to urn:* This is a minority view that continues to be put forward —see William R. Wood, *English Journal*, XXIX (1940), 837–39; Roy P. Basler, *Explicator*, IV (1945), item 6; Porter Williams, Jr., *Modern Language Notes*, LXX (1955), 342–45; and especially Martin Halpern, *College English*, XXIV (1963), 284–88. The poet's final words are read as a comment on the urn's limitations: in Basler's paraphrase, "That is all you . . . know, and all you need to know; but, I know a great deal more, and a different quality of beauty and truth." *Objections:* "Ye" is normally a plural pronoun. And the urn has been referred to as "thou" throughout the poem. (Halpern cites instances of singular "ye," as well as shifts of pronouns, elsewhere in Keats's poems. A number of critics suggest that Keats may have changed pronouns to avoid the cacophony of "that is all / Thou knowest on earth, and all thou needest to know.") "On earth" in the last line is meaningless if applied to the urn.

(3) *Poet to figures on the urn:* This (proposed by G. St. Quintin, *Times Literary Supplement*, February 5, 1938, p. 92, and more recently by Robert Berkelman, *South Atlantic Quarterly*, LVII [1958], 354–58) is a variety of the preceding, but better accords with the normal use of "ye" as a plural. *Objections:* The figures are not "on earth." Moreover, the poet has ceased to think of them as alive and capable of hearing; he is again addressing the urn as artifact, and the images of the last stanza emphasize the lifelessness of "marble men and maidens." And there is no reason why the figures should know only "Beauty . . . beauty," or anything at all.

(4) *Urn to reader:* The commonest view of the conclusion of the ode—popularized by Cleanth Brooks and C. M. Bowra in the 1940's, reinforced by the solid stand of the Harvard Keatsians, Douglas Bush, W. J. Bate, and David Perkins, and seemingly sanctioned by the punctuation in the transcripts—has the urn speaking the whole of the last two lines. *Objections:* There is again the question of common-sense meaning (though it seems better for the urn to tell us what we know and need to know than for the poet to do so). The principal obstacle, however, is the punctuation of the text in the *Lamia* volume. Several critics (e.g., R. D. Havens, *Modern Philology*, XXIV [1926], 213; Leo Spitzer, *Comparative Literature*, VII [1955], 220–21) have suggested that the quotation marks may have been intended to set off "Beauty . . . beauty" as an apothegm, motto, or sepulchral epigram. Bush (e.g., in his *Selected Poems and Letters*, 1959) and others, rejecting the *Lamia* punctuation, simply move the closing quotation mark to the end of the poem.

# Chronology of Events

|  | *Keats* | *The Age* |
|---|---|---|
| 1795 | John Keats is born in London on October 31, the eldest son of Thomas Keats, manager of a livery stable, and Frances Jennings. Subsequent children are George (1797–1841), Thomas (1799–1818), Edward (1801, dies in infancy), and Frances Mary, called Fanny (1803–89). | |
| 1798 | | Wordsworth's and Coleridge's *Lyrical Ballads.* |
| 1803–11 | With George and, later, Tom, attends Clarke's school at Enfield, north of London. | |
| 1804 | His father dies in a riding accident in April. His mother remarries in June, and the children go to live with their grandparents. | |
| 1805 | | The Battle of Trafalgar. |
| 1807 | | Wordsworth's *Poems in Two Volumes.* |
| 1808 | | Goethe's *Faust,* Part I. |
| 1810 | His mother dies of tuberculosis in March. | |
| 1811–15 | Apprenticeship to an apothecary-surgeon at Edmonton. | The Regency (1811–20). |
| 1812 | | Byron's *Childe Harold,* Cantos I and II. |
| 1814 | Writes earliest poems (beginning with *Imitation of Spenser*). | Wordsworth's *The Excursion.* |
| 1815 | Enters Guy's Hospital, London, in October to begin further medical training. | Napoleon defeated at Waterloo. |

| *Keats* | *The Age* |
|---|---|
| 1816 | His first published poem (the sonnet *O Solitude!*) appears in May. Passes apothecaries' examination in July. Accelerated poetic activity beginning in August. | Shelley's *Alastor*; Coleridge's *Christabel, Kubla Khan, and The Pains of Sleep;* Byron's *Childe Harold,* Canto III. |
| 1817 | His first volume, *Poems,* published in March. Embarks on *Endymion* in April. | Coleridge's *Biographia Literaria* and *Sibylline Leaves.* |
| 1818 | Writes *Isabella* (February–April). *Endymion* published in April. George Keats and his bride emigrate to America in June. Walking tour through northern England and Scotland in June–August. Begins *Hyperion* in September. Meets Fanny Brawne. Tom Keats dies of tuberculosis in December. | Shelley's *The Revolt of Islam;* Byron's *Childe Harold,* Canto IV |
| 1819 | Writes the poems that put him "among the English Poets": *The Eve of St. Agnes* (January–February), *La Belle Dame sans Merci* (April), the odes—*Psyche, Nightingale, Grecian Urn, Melancholy* (April–May), *Lamia* and *The Fall of Hyperion* (July–September), *To Autumn* (September). | Byron's *Don Juan,* Cantos I and II. |
| 1820 | Severe hemorrhage in the lungs in February (the final illness now under way). His third volume, *Lamia, Isabella, The Eve of St. Agnes, and Other Poems,* published in July. Sails for Italy in September. | Death of George III. Shelley's *Prometheus Unbound.* |
| 1821 | Dies in Rome on February 23. | Shelley's *Epipsychidion* and *Adonais.* |

# Selected Bibliography

## Bibliographical Guides

Green, David Bonnell, and Edwin Graves Wilson, eds., *Keats, Shelley, Byron, Hunt, and Their Circles: A Bibliography* (Lincoln: University of Nebraska Press, 1964)—an indexed reprint of the first twelve *Keats-Shelley Journal* annual bibliographies, covering 1950–62.

MacGillivray, J. R., *Keats: A Bibliography and Reference Guide* (Toronto: University of Toronto Press, 1949).

Thorpe, Clarence D., "Keats," *The English Romantic Poets: A Review of Research*, ed. Thomas M. Raysor, revised edn. (New York: Modern Language Association, 1956).

See also the annual bibliographies of research in *PMLA* (1922–  ), *ELH* (1937–49), *Philological Quarterly* (1950–64), *English Language Notes* (1965–  ), and *Keats-Shelley Journal* (1952–  ).

## Editions

*The Poetical Works of John Keats*, ed. H. W. Garrod (Oxford: Clarendon Press, 1939; 2nd edn., 1958)—the standard edition.

*Selected Poems and Letters*, ed. Douglas Bush (Boston: Houghton Mifflin Company, 1959).

*The Letters of John Keats*, ed. Hyder Edward Rollins, 2 vols. (Cambridge, Mass.: Harvard University Press, 1958).

*The Keats Circle: Letters and Papers, 1816–1878*, ed. Hyder Edward Rollins, 2 vols. (Cambridge, Mass.: Harvard University Press, 1948; 2nd edn., 1965).

## Biographies

Bate, Walter Jackson, *John Keats* (Cambridge, Mass.: Harvard University Press, 1963).

Colvin, Sidney, *John Keats: His Life and Poetry, His Friends, Critics, and After-Fame* (London: Macmillan & Co., Ltd., 1917; 3rd edn., 1920).

Gittings, Robert, *John Keats* (Boston and Toronto: Little, Brown and Company, 1968).

Hewlett, Dorothy, *Adonais: A Life of John Keats* (London: Hurst & Blackett Limited, 1937; 2nd edn., *A Life of John Keats,* 1949).

Lowell, Amy, *John Keats,* 2 vols. (Boston and New York: Houghton Mifflin Company, 1925).

Ward, Aileen, *John Keats: The Making of a Poet* (New York: Viking Press, 1963).

See also the chronology of "Events in the Life of Keats" in Rollins' edition of *The Letters,* I, 29–61.

## Selected Criticism

Bate, Walter Jackson, ed., *Keats: A Collection of Critical Essays* (Englewood Cliffs, N.J.: Prentice-Hall, Inc., 1964)—reprints discussions of the odes by Bloom, Perkins, Wasserman, and Bate.

Bate, Walter Jackson, *The Stylistic Development of Keats* (New York: Modern Language Association, 1945)—metrical analysis, with statistics and intelligent commentary.

Bloom, Harold, *The Visionary Company: A Reading of English Romantic Poetry* (Garden City, N.Y.: Doubleday & Company, Inc., 1961)—contains original and acute explications of the five odes.

Bowra, C. M., "Ode on a Grecian Urn," *The Romantic Imagination* (Cambridge, Mass.: Harvard University Press, 1949)—reads the poem as Keats's theory of art.

Brooks, Cleanth, "History without Footnotes: An Account of Keats' Urn," *Sewanee Review,* LII (1944), 89–101; reprinted in *The Well Wrought Urn* (New York: Reynal & Company, Inc., 1947)—on the dramatic appropriateness of the final lines; like the next item, a brilliant and influential essay, widely anthologized.

Burke, Kenneth, "Symbolic Action in a Poem by Keats," *Accent,* IV (1943), 30–42; reprinted in *A Grammar of Motives* (New York: Prentice-Hall, Inc., 1945)—reads *Ode on a Grecian Urn* as a proclamation of the unity of science and art.

Bush, Douglas, *John Keats: His Life and Writings* (New York: The Macmillan Company, 1966)—the distilled wisdom of several decades' familiarity with the poems; like the next item (as well as Bush's *Selected Poems and Letters*), especially illuminating on Keats's sources and his ideas.

Bush, Douglas, "Keats," *Mythology and the Romantic Tradition in English Poetry* (Cambridge, Mass.: Harvard University Press, 1937).

Finney, Claude Lee, *The Evolution of Keats's Poetry,* 2 vols. (Cambridge, Mass.: Harvard University Press, 1936)—a standard work on sources, influences, biographical facts, and interpretation.

Fogle, Richard Harter, *The Imagery of Keats and Shelley* (Chapel Hill:

University of North Carolina Press, 1949)—includes discussion of synaesthetic and empathic imagery in the odes.

Ford, Newell F., *The Prefigurative Imagination of John Keats*, Stanford University Publications, Language and Literature, IX (Stanford: Stanford University Press, 1951)—an important study focusing on the Beauty–Truth identification in *Ode on a Grecian Urn*.

Garrod, H. W., *Keats* (Oxford: Clarendon Press, 1926; 2nd edn., 1939)—contains valuable comments on the development of the ode from Keats's experiments with the sonnet.

Harrison, Thomas P., "Keats and a Nightingale," *English Studies*, XLI (1960), 353–59—relates the bird's song to the movements of the poem.

Holloway, John, "The Odes of Keats," *Cambridge Journal*, V (1952), 416–25; reprinted in *The Charted Mirror* (London: Routledge & Kegan Paul Ltd., 1960)—general analysis of the odes as a unified sequence.

Lyon, Harvey T., *Keats' Well-Read Urn* (New York: Holt, Rinehart & Winston, Inc., 1958)—a collection of critical commentary from the 1820's through 1957.

McLuhan, Herbert Marshall, "Aesthetic Pattern in Keats's Odes," *University of Toronto Quarterly*, XII (1943), 167–79—on "down" and "up" movements in *Ode to a Nightingale*.

Muir, Kenneth, ed., *John Keats: A Reassessment* (Liverpool: Liverpool University Press, 1958)—includes essays on the odes by Muir, Allott, and Arnold Davenport.

Murry, John Middleton, *Keats* (London: Jonathan Cape Limited, 1955)—contains a chapter on the final lines of *Ode on a Grecian Urn*.

Perkins, David, "Keats's Odes and Letters: Recurrent Diction and Imagery," *Keats-Shelley Journal*, II (1953), 51–60.

Perkins, David, *The Quest for Permanence: The Symbolism of Wordsworth, Shelley, and Keats* (Cambridge, Mass.: Harvard University Press, 1959)—excellent discussion of Keats's attitudes toward process, permanence, and the visionary imagination.

Ridley, M. R., *Keats' Craftsmanship* (Oxford: Clarendon Press, 1933)—on Keats's verbal "carpentry" as revealed by successive revisions in the manuscripts.

Shackford, Martha Hale, "The *Ode on a Grecian Urn*," *Keats-Shelley Journal*, IV (1955), 7–13—reads the poem as a Platonic hymn in praise of beauty.

Southam, B. C., "The Ode 'To Autumn,'" *Keats-Shelley Journal*, IX (1960), 91–98—general analysis.

Spens, Janet, "A Study of Keats's 'Ode to a Nightingale,'" *Review of English Studies*, new ser., III (1952), 234–43—finds sources of the poem in Hazlitt's *Lectures on the English Poets*.

Spitzer, Leo, "The 'Ode on a Grecian Urn,' or Content vs. Metagrammar," *Comparative Literature*, VII (1955), 203–25—an attack on Wasserman's critical methods.

Tate, Allen, "A Reading of Keats," *American Scholar,* XV (1945–46), 55–63, 189–97; reprinted in *On the Limits of Poetry* (New York: Swallow Press, 1948)—mainly on *Ode to a Nightingale* and the inadequacy of Keats's language to the experience he was trying to write about.

Wasserman, Earl R., *The Finer Tone: Keats' Major Poems* (Baltimore: The Johns Hopkins Press, 1953)—contains chapters on *Grecian Urn* and *Nightingale;* a brilliant work, and a principal stimulus to some of the best Keats criticism of the decade following its publication.

# Notes on Contributors

JACK STILLINGER, the editor of this volume, is Professor of English at the University of Illinois. He has published articles on Keats, Sidney, and J. S. Mill, among others, and has edited a draft of Mill's *Autobiography* (1961), Anthony Munday's *Zelauto* (1963), a selection of Wordsworth (1965), and the letters of Charles Armitage Brown (1966).

M. H. ABRAMS, Professor of English at Cornell University, is the author of *The Milk of Paradise* (1934) and *The Mirror and the Lamp* (1953), and editor of *The Norton Anthology of English Literature* (1962).

KENNETH ALLOTT, Andrew Cecil Bradley Professor of English Literature in the University of Liverpool, has written studies of Jules Verne (1940), Matthew Arnold (1955), and Graham Greene (1963), and has edited the poems of William Habington (1948) and Arnold (1965).

WALTER JACKSON BATE, Abbott Lawrence Lowell Professor of the Humanities at Harvard University, has published, among other works, *The Stylistic Development of Keats* (1945), *From Classic to Romantic* (1946), *The Achievement of Samuel Johnson* (1955), *John Keats* (1963), and *Coleridge* (1968).

F. W. BATESON, Fellow and Tutor in English Literature, Corpus Christi College, Oxford, is the author of several books on English poetry, including *Wordsworth: A Re-interpretation* (1954), and the editor of *Essays in Criticism*.

HAROLD BLOOM, Professor of English at Yale, has written *Shelley's Mythmaking* (1959), *The Visionary Company* (1961), *Blake's Apocalypse* (1963), and the commentary for David Erdman's edition of Blake (1965).

CLEANTH BROOKS, Gray Professor of Rhetoric at Yale University, has written, among other works, *Modern Poetry and the Tradition* (1939), *The Well Wrought Urn* (1947), *The Hidden God* (1963), and *William Faulkner* (1963).

DOUGLAS BUSH, Gurney Professor of English at Harvard, has published important works in almost every field of English literature. His principal contributions to the study of Keats are *Mythology and the Romantic Tradition in English Poetry* (1937), his edition of Keats's *Selected Poems and Letters* (1959), and *John Keats: His Life and Writings* (1966).

RICHARD HARTER FOGLE, Professor of English at the University of North Carolina, is the author of *The Imagery of Keats and Shelley* (1949), *Hawthorne's Fiction* (1952), *Melville's Shorter Tales* (1960), and *The Idea of Coleridge's Criticism* (1962).

ALBERT GÉRARD, Advanced Fellow in the National Foundation for Scientific Research, Brussels, is the author of *L'idée romantique de la poésie en Angleterre* (1955) and many essays in English and comparative literature.

ANTHONY HECHT, Professor of English at Bard College, has published several volumes of poetry, beginning with *A Summoning of Stones* (1954).

LEONIDAS M. JONES, Professor of English at the University of Vermont, has published articles on Keats and J. H. Reynolds and an edition of Reynolds' *Selected Prose* (1966).

CHARLES I. PATTERSON, Professor of English at the University of Georgia, has published articles on Coleridge, Hazlitt, De Quincey, Wordsworth, and others.

DAVID PERKINS, Professor of English at Harvard, is the author of *The Quest for Permanence* (1959) and *Wordsworth and the Poetry of Sincerity* (1964), and editor of an anthology of Romantic literature (1967).

LEONARD UNGER, Professor of English at the University of Minnesota, has published *Donne's Poetry and Modern Criticism* (1950) and several studies of T. S. Eliot.

ROBERT PENN WARREN, the distinguished poet, novelist, and critic, is Professor of English at Yale.

JACOB WIGOD, Associate Professor of English at the University of British Columbia, has published essays on Negative Capability and *Endymion*.

# TWENTIETH CENTURY
# INTERPRETATIONS

MAYNARD MACK, *Series Editor*
Yale University

NOW AVAILABLE
*Collections of Critical Essays*
ON